Psychoanalysis and the Human Sciences

—

EUROPEAN PERSPECTIVES:

A SERIES IN SOCIAL THOUGHT

AND CULTURAL CRITICISM

Psychoanalysis and the Human Sciences

—

Louis Althusser

Translated by Steven Rendall

COLUMBIA UNIVERSITY PRESS | NEW YORK

Columbia University Press
Publishers Since 1893
New York   Chichester, West Sussex
cup.columbia.edu
Copyright © 1996 Librairie Générale Française/IMEC
Published by special arrangement with La Librairie Générale Française in
conjunction with their duly appointed agent, 2 Seas Literary Agency.
English translation copyright © 2016 Columbia University Press
All rights reserved

Library of Congress Cataloging-in-Publication Data
Names: Althusser, Louis, 1918–1990, author.
Title: Psychoanalysis and the human sciences / Louis Althusser ; translated
    by Steven Rendall.
Description: New York : Columbia University Press, 2016. | Series: European
    perspectives : a series in social thought and cultural criticism |
    Includes bibliographical references and index.
Identifiers : LCCN 2016001256| ISBN 9780231177641 (cloth : alk. paper) |
    ISBN 9780231177658 (pbk. : alk. paper) | ISBN 9780231542104 (e-book)
Subjects: LCSH: Psychoanalysis—Philosophy. | Psychology—Philosophy. |
    Lacan, Jacques, 1901–1981.
Classification: LCC BF173 .A63 2016 | DDC 150. 19/5—dc23
LC record available at https://lccn.loc.gov/2016001256

Columbia University Press books are printed on permanent and durable
acid-free paper.
Printed in the United States of America
c 10 9 8 7 6 5 4 3 2 1
p 10 9 8 7 6 5 4 3 2 1

Cover design: Lisa Hamm

Contents

Foreword   vii

Pascale Gillot

Editor's Preface   xxix

Olivier Corpet and François Matheron

1   The Place of Psychoanalysis in the Human Sciences   1

2   Psychoanalysis and Psychology   45

Notes   89

Index   97

Foreword

Pascale Gillot

THESE TWO talks given by Louis Althusser in 1963–1964, in the context of an ENS seminar on the question of psychoanalysis seen from Jacques Lacan's perspective, deal with the topic of the *problematic scientificity of the human sciences* in general. They are of strategic interest not only because they first reveal, just before the article "Freud and Lacan" was published in 1964–1965,[1] the deep intellectual influence exerted by Lacan's thought on Althusser's own theoretical task in these years—the *return to Marx*, which involved a struggle against psychologism as well as against any philosophy of consciousness, but also because they involve a concept at stake in Althusser's philosophical program of elaborating a theory of *ideology* in general—the concept of the *subject*.

The Question of the Human Sciences: A Central Philosophical Issue

It is well known that the question of the human sciences and their scientific status lay at the heart of French philosophical reflection in the second half of the twentieth century.[2]

When Althusser gave these two talks, he saw the problematic character of the human sciences—that is, their *uncertain scientificity*—as characterized by their oscillation between science and ideology or technique. This problem may be considered central for philosophy, considered as theoretical philosophy, by contrast with what Althusser sometimes calls "ideological philosophy," namely subjectivist and existential philosophy.

An almost contemporary article called "Philosophy and the Human Sciences" sheds light on what at stake in this problem of the epistemology of the human sciences insofar as philosophy is concerned.[3]

In "Philosophy and the Human Sciences" Althusser denounces contemporary philosophy's continuing "predilection" for psychology even after the decay of spiritualism and Bergsonism. He also underlines a crucial reason why the "human sciences" are still not real sciences: the strange persistence of the philosophical notion of a "radical transcendence of the Subject." Phenomenology, represented in the early 1960s by Sartre and Merleau-Ponty—whose phenomenology is very remote from the original Husserlian insight—is the main target of Althusser's attack, so far as it had become the mask for a philosophy of consciousness and of the subject. He suggests that the domination of this philosophical trend explains the unstable and unsatisfying situation of the human sciences, their lack of genuine scientificity. In contrast, Althusser calls for an autonomous philosophy based upon the rejection of "positivism," "empiricism," "psychologism," and "pragmatism."

Philosophy in general may thus be conceived as a double of the human sciences. One might therefore expect Althusser to assert the common destiny of philosophy and the human sciences, *against empiricism, positivism, and psychologism,* which together form an *ideology* generally identified with "empiricist ideology." This ideology represents the adversary of philosophy considered as theory and not as ideology. More precisely, Althusser assigns to philosophy the epistemological task of "reflecting on the reality of scientific practice." Consequently, once the myth of the sciences' spontaneous comprehension of their own practice has been set aside, an important object of philosophical investigation is reflection on the specific scientificity of the human sciences, these "disciplines that call themselves sciences." Therefore, philosophy's general scope does not consist in the rejection of the "objectivity" of the human sciences but, on the contrary, in the attempt to give them conceptual tools that can help them recognize their own possibility as sciences and fully achieve scientificity.

However we must note that Althusser generally sees "philosophy" as occupying an ambiguous position *between theory and ideology*—like the human sciences themselves. Hence the constant denunciation of this *ideological philosophy* (existentialism, personalism, subjectivism) identified as "pseudo phenomenology," a legacy of Bergsonian spiritualism, which he calls the ally of "technocratic ideology." Thus Althusser draws a clear dividing line between this ideological philosophy and a theoretical philosophy—which he adopts as his own position—conceived as an antiempiricist and antipsychologistic reflection on scientific practice: what was later called a "philosophy of the concept."

In that conflictual context, the role of nonideological philosophy is said to consist in defending the human sciences against what prevents them from being truly scientific, in permitting their transformation from their current status of *techniques*—human techniques—to the status of genuine *sciences*. Consequently it involves freeing the human sciences from technocratic ideology, whose correlatives are subjectivism, anthropologism, and psychologism.

The general perspective adopted by Althusser in 1963, just before these two talks, thus appears to be a *critical perspective* on the situation of the so-called human sciences at that time—human sciences whose scientificity was still to come and were for the most part mere techniques for adapting or readapting individuals to their social milieu: "Human Techniques of Adaptation" disguised as sciences. *Linguistics*, Althusser insists, is a remarkable exception, it is a *real science* with a specific object and a specific method. But other so-called sciences, such as contemporary sociology and psychology, or psychosociology, are nothing but techniques for gaining social control over individuals; they are still pseudo-sciences.

In this respect, it is conceivable that psychoanalysis, taking linguistics as its model, might also constitute a precious paradigm of scientificity in the domain of the human sciences, insofar as it could be seen as built on a rejection of psychology. And this is where Lacan comes in. He addresses this question of the complex relation between psychoanalysis and psychology, which involves the possibility that psychoanalysis can form a genuine theory, a genuine science, and not a mere intersubjective practice, by making a radical break with the tradition of psychology: a break entailed by the Freudian concept of the unconscious. This concept may be considered strategic insofar as it allows us to build *a bridge with the human sciences,* in the rigorous sense of the word, and with their "objective reality." These sciences are related to a certain conception of the unconscious, namely the unconscious as the structures that determine the laws of the anthropological sphere—like modern linguistics, which postulates the unconscious character of the laws that govern the human use of language. This understanding of psychoanalysis as the theory of the unconscious is developed by Lacan precisely through his recourse to linguistics and structural analysis.[4]

The Complex History of Freud's Reception in French Philosophy in the Twentieth Century

In the first talk, Althusser develops a historical reconstruction of the introduction of Freudian psychoanalysis into French thought, and specifically into French philosophy. Such a historical perspective is striking in two ways.

First, it offers an autobiographical retrospective through which Althusser shows the importance that phenomenology had in his own philosophical formation, before he departed from it. He emphasizes the important role played by Merleau-Ponty, Sartre, and also Ricoeur in the initial reception of psychoanalysis within French philosophy. All these authors were deeply influenced by Georges Politzer, who introduced Freudian psychoanalysis into French philosophy. Politzer's crucial reading of Freud's theory in the *Critique des fondements de la psychologie* (1928) identified psychoanalysis as the path toward "concrete psychology." We should note that this historical inquiry includes Althusser's description of his own encounter with psychoanalysis through Politzer's interpretation, and leads to a *retrospective critique* of his initial understanding of Freud's attempt to depart from classical psychology. The main issue at stake is the adequate conception of the distinction or *break* between psychoanalysis and classical psychology.

But this historical reconstruction also helps us understand the premises of the antagonism—so important in twentieth-century French philosophy—between structural analysis and phenomenology, or between a "philosophy of the concept" and a "philosophy of consciousness." Some years later, this antagonistic configuration was defined by Michel Foucault as a dividing line that separates a "philosophy of experience, of sense and of the subject" from a "philosophy of knowledge, of rationality and of the concept."[5] The philosophy of the concept involves a strong antipsychologistic claim, and, in the context of such a struggle,

Jacques Lacan, who was an obstinate and ferocious adversary of psychology and opposed to any attempt to obliterate the dividing line between psychoanalysis and psychology, represents a precious ally. In that respect, Lacan's perspective concerning the irreducibility of Freud's theory with respect to psychology is closely related to Georges Canguilhem's attack on psychology, its instrumentalism and its false pretension to constitute a *science*, in the famous 1956 article entitled "Qu'est-ce que la psychologie?" ("What Is Psychology?").[6]

The second version of Althusser's historical reconstruction deals with the topic that gives the volume its title: the relation between psychoanalysis and the human sciences—anthropology, sociology—and *psychology*.

The crucial examination of the relation of psychoanalysis to psychology is inserted within a consideration of the broader encounter of psychoanalysis with social psychology, psychiatry, and anthropology that began in Freud's time and indicates the necessity of the historical move leading psychoanalysis toward the "general object of the human sciences." It is in this framework that Althusser examines the symbiosis, in 1963, between psychoanalysis and psychology in the "current state of the social sciences"—a symbiosis that takes the particular form of the psychoanalysis of children, in relation to the psychology of child development and to the different theories of its "phases" or "stages."

This historical importance of the theory of child development reveals a conception of psychoanalysis that is inadequate, insofar as it is still framed by anthropologism, and not yet scientific.

More precisely, it appears to be governed by an idealist conception of the encounter between the individual and society, or "social praxis," and to imply a misunderstanding concerning the object of psychoanalysis identified in the interaction between the individual—considered as the biological individual—and the "social milieu." This configuration leads to the reduction of psychoanalysis to a technique of social adaptation that was the object of a constant critique by Lacan, under the name of "American psychoanalysis," which he considered as "the exact opposite of psychoanalysis," as Althusser puts it.

The first historical encounter between psychoanalysis and human sciences such as psychology, anthropology, and psychiatry, seems therefore to be characterized by anthropologism and psychologism, i.e., by idealist determinations that prevent the human sciences from achieving scientificity.

In contrast, the new program established by Althusser, which requires Lacan's decisive contribution, would make possible a renewal of the encounter between psychoanalysis and the human sciences, an epistemological reflection on their articulation emancipated from anthropologism and psychologism. This would also mean a real encounter between psychoanalysis and philosophy, based on a radical redefinition of psychoanalysis itself and of its own scientificity.

For it happens, Althusser explains, that the first encounter between philosophy and psychoanalysis occurred under the jurisdiction of Sartre and Merleau-Ponty, and implied a false conception of the respective functions of these two domains. According to this conception, psychoanalysis would provide the *concrete*, the material: in the present case, the intersubjective situation of therapy (*la cure*) or, in other words, the "dual situation of the relation between doctor and patient." The insistence on the existential surroundings of psychoanalysis identifies the latter as a *practice,* a therapeutic practice that lacks its own concepts, whereas philosophy is supposed to provide the *concepts*. Psychoanalysis would thus be reduced to a mere empirical practice and would therefore not be able to constitute itself as a *science*.

One understands better in this light Lacan's (and Althusser's) recurrent denunciation of the "theoretical imposture" represented by the philosophical interpretation of the *intersubjectivity* supposedly at work in the psychoanalytical experience of therapy, their rejection of the phenomenological focus put on the double relationship between patient and doctor. This explains the intensity of the controversy engaged not only against Sartre and Merleau-Ponty but also, in a more implicit way, against Ricoeur himself and his "philosophy of intersubjectivity."

The Exportation of Lacan's Thought Into the Domain of Philosophy

One could sum up the theoretical debt that explicitly links Althusser to Lacan—starting from the text of 1963, "Philosophy and the Human Sciences," continuing through these two talks, and still at work in the article "Freud and Lacan" in 1964—in the following schematic points. Lacan's return to Freud reveals that psychoanalysis invalidates the myth of the *homo psychologicus*, just as Marx's theory read by Althusser invalidates the myth of the *homo oeconomicus*. In this regard, Althusser wrote in "Philosophy and the Human Sciences," regarding Lacan, "We owe him what is *essential*."

Lacan's insight about the scientificity of psychoanalysis, entailed by the claim that it has made an epistemological break with psychology, is a model for the definition of the specific scientificity of the human sciences in general, particularly with regard to historical materialism.

Lacan's insistent questioning about the specific status of psychoanalysis is taken up by Althusser from the beginning, but in a specific way; it is *exported to the domain of philosophy*. That is the object of the title and of the *incipit* of the first talk: the reading and the interpretation of Lacan are immediately subordinated to the epistemological topic of the *human sciences*, considered through the prism of psychoanalysis.

The central question, inherited from Lacan, is thus: what is the essence of psychoanalysis, and what is its specific, scientific, object?

This question thus concerns the theoretical status of psychoanalysis. It was first formulated by Lacan against the tradition of a psychology of consciousness and resolved in the pungent critique of any reduction of psychoanalysis to an existential experience that would take the form of an intersubjective process.

This question underpins Althusser's philosophical reflection on the theoretical status of the human sciences in general and the possibility that they might escape the ideological field in which they were born and with which they have to break in order to constitute themselves as sciences: i.e., subjectivism and psychologism.

Thus Althusser's resumption of Lacan's reading of Freud suggests that reflection on the epistemology of psychoanalysis leads to reflection on the epistemology of the human sciences.

This might help us better understand Athusser's insistence on what might at first seem a disconcerting task: *translating Lacan*— a task that is described as "a very important cultural necessity" at the end of the first talk. Through this programmatic statement, Althusser expresses the wish to *make Lacan's thought operate in the field of philosophy*, to extract it from the baroque envelope that seems to characterize it as long as it remains in the closed realm of the practicians of psychoanalysis. Indeed, Lacan's attempt to give a coherent, *theoretical* definition of the essence of psychoanalysis is strategic with regard to "the whole domain of the human sciences" in general—together with Marxism and "the problematics inaugurated by Marx": the two theoretical "points of departure," the "mooring-points." This definition of the essence of psychoanalysis is essential for the understanding of the "relation *de jure* between psychoanalysis and the human sciences."

Once again, Althusser's investigation deals with the epistemological specificity of psychoanalysis considered not as a therapeutics or an existential intersubjective apparatus but as a *theory*: the theory of the unconscious as such. Here Althusser seems to be following Lacan's reading of Freud, which aimed at isolating the specific *scientificity* of psychoanalysis at stake in Freud's discovery concerning the *concept* of unconscious, against regressive readings by the followers of the "ego psychology" theorized by Anna Freud and the representatives of "American psychoanalysis." The critique of the trend to absorb psychoanalysis within psychology is repeated in the second talk, in relation to the question of the separation of psychoanalysis from psychology. Althusser refers to Lacan's rejection of a "psychological theory of the unconscious." The latter is particularly represented by what he sees as Anna Freud's misinterpretation when, reading Freud's second representation of the psychic apparatus (the ego, the id, the superego), she reactivated the notion of the psychological subject, the supposed *centrality* of the "ego." For Althusser, the core of the misunderstanding consists in Anna Freud's rechanneling of the *psychological subject* conceived through the form of the centered ego, "the "ego" being the central position that tries to remain central, that tries to maintain its position against the aggressions of the "id" or of "social reality." This leads to an instrumentalist and theoretically misleading conception of psychoanalysis—typical of American psychoanalysis—that consists in the reduction of psychoanalysis to a "technique of readaptation" of the individuals to the social context in which they live and to the norms to which they are supposed to conform.

The main issues at stake in this general reflection on the relation of philosophy to the human sciences are therefore the epistemological distinction between science and ideology and the parallel *distinction between psychoanalysis and psychology*, a question that represents the core of the second conference, entitled "Psychoanalysis and Psychology."

These texts by Althusser, so deeply informed by Lacan's work, might also be read as a laboratory for the concept of "epistemological break" (*la coupure épistémologique*). This concept, borrowed from Bachelard's epistemology, makes possible a distinction between science and ideology, and its use will be determinant in Althusser's later texts (*For Marx* and *Reading Capital*, in 1965) in the context of the "return to Marx." These texts are concerned with the scientificity of Marxism and historical materialism in the context of Marx's revolutionary discovery, the discovery of the continent History, leading to the constitution of historical materialism: a scientificity that must be constructed on the rigorous distinction between the young Marx's writings, still influenced by Feuerbachian humanist ideology, Hegelian idealist philosophy, and classical political economy, on the one hand, and on the other Marx's mature works such as *Capital*, freed from anthropologism and historical teleology, after the "break" represented by *The German Ideology* in 1845.

Lacan's return to Freud is exemplary in that respect. It is a decisive attempt to transform and systematize, within the theoretical field of psychoanalysis, the conceptual apparatus inherited from Freud, and to reveal the "epistemological break" through which psychoanalysis emancipates itself from its ideological background. In Freud, most concepts are still borrowed or "imported," they are inherited from theoretical areas that form the prehistory of psychoanalysis: biology, energetistic physics, economic theory. Lacan transformed these borrowed concepts into "domestic ones" (according to Kant's distinction), having recourse to *linguistics* and its epistemological framework, that is, structural analysis, which deeply inspired Lacan's reading of Freud in the 1950s.

The analogy between Lacan's strategy and Althusser's some years later is particularly significant on this epistemological level, and it could explain Althusser's insistence on what he sometimes calls his debt (as a philosopher and as a Marxist philosopher) to Lacan.

The Premises to the Theory of Ideology

These analyses of the analogy between the return to Freud and the return to Marx lead us to another crucial point of encounter of Althusser with Lacan, i.e., the *conceptualization of ideology*, which involves and requires two different origins: Spinoza's materialism of the imaginary and—what interests us most here—Freud's concept of the unconscious as it was reread and systematized by Lacan himself in the *Ecrits*.[7]

The elements for a theory of ideology borrowed from the Freudian-Lacanian perspective in connection with a theory of the process of humanization-subjectivization are systematically delivered one year later in the article "Freud and Lacan" and determine the further systematization of the theory of ideology as such in *Ideology and Ideological State Apparatuses*, a text written in 1970.[8]

But it is already possible to track down some decisive premises of these theoretical elements in the talks themselves, particularly in the second one.

Let us recall first that in *Ideology and Ideological State Apparatuses* Althusser asserts his central theoretical program to develop a *theory of ideology* in general, on the model of Freud's *theory of* the *Unconscious*. Thus, far from being reducible to the illusory domain of conscious representations, ideas, etc., that is, to the simple inversion of "real life," ideology is endowed with a necessity, an omnihistorical character, and a "material reality" that proceed from its necessary inscription in social institutions ("ideological state apparatuses" such as family, army, church, etc.) and also from the fact that its own causal effectiveness is comparable to the causal effectiveness of the unconscious, conceived in the Freudian way as an independent system. This explains why ideology, as Althusser already underscored in *For Marx*, cannot be eliminated from any social formation: it is an *"essential structure"* of human societies in general.[9]

Hence the definition: "an ideology is a system (with its own logic and rigor) of representations (images, myths, ideas, or concepts, depending on the case) endowed with a historical existence and role within a given society."[10]

This characteristic of ideological reality also entails that human life, the life of human individuals, is necessarily in the grip of ideology. Human beings are in this sense "ideological animals," which means that they are always already assigned to become subjects: subjected to the "law of culture," the other name for the necessity and power of ideology in all social formations.

According to this approach to ideology—directed against the pre-Marxian conception of ideology as a mere fantastic inversion of reality, deprived of any form of specific reality and effectiveness—the fundamental mechanism of ideology is what Althusser calls the "interpellation into subject," the *subjectivization-subjection process.*[11]

Now, this later theorization of the ideological function is deeply marked by Lacan's definition of the object of psychoanalysis as being the *humanization process*, the humanization of the little human child: "the little child's becoming human, his integration into culture through the defiles of the signifier," in Althusser's words. Thus it refers to the claim of the constant precession of the *symbolic function* with regard to the humanization-subjectivation process. And light is shed on this Lacanian conception of the primacy of the symbolic order by the Rousseauist concept of the "law of culture." Together with Lacan,

Rousseau operates, with his *Discours sur l'origine et les fonde-ments de l'ingalité parmi les hommes,* as a decisive ally *against* the ideological-psychological representation of the humanization process that supposes the continuity of the passage to human-ization: a classical representation that was at the core of eigh-teenth-century reflection (see Condillac) on "wild children," for example. Through Rousseau's paradoxical claim of the disconti-nuity between nature and culture, we are led to understand the necessity of culture's self-precession, i.e., the antecedence of the symbolic order (antecedent to the imaginary order itself) with respect to all the "stages" of human development.

Althusser's use of Lacan's concept of the symbolic order and of Rousseau's concept of the "law of culture" thus appears to be rather original: he chooses to link them together in order to work out the crucial claim that was to be at the core of his own theory of ideology: namely *culture's self-precession*, its constant and necessary antecedence with respect to the humanization-subjectivization process.

What the alliance between Lacan and Rousseau makes it pos-sible to conceive is therefore the inadequacy of the traditional representation (inherent in ego psychology or the classical psy-chology of child development) of the humanization process as a *passage from nature to culture*, from the biological to the cultural-social-anthropological sphere.

In opposition to this representation of the subject as psy-chological subject, a subject of needs, and the representation of

language as a tool for communication between individuals—
a mediation used by the psychological subject to signify his
needs to the other subjects—the reference to Lacan's perspective sketches out a different perspective based upon *modern linguistics*, which implies the opposite claim that entails a whole
(antipsychologistic) theory of the subject, conceived not as the
imaginary ego (the ego of consciousness) but as the symbolic
subject, a subject in the grip of language.

As a result, Rousseau and Lacan, both of whom conceptualize "this precession of culture with respect to itself," provide the
foundations for the strategic refutation of philosophical individualism (Hobbes) and for the disqualification of experimental psychology and psychology in general. This Lacanian-Rousseauist
refutation could be understood as the conceptual basis for the
double rejection of the *homo oeconomicus* and of the *homo psychologicus*: two ideological figures that together form a system. In
its turn, such a rejection might constitute a central precondition
for the elaboration of the human *sciences* as such, a precondition
for their break with ideology and technocratic thought that rely
on anthropologism, individualism, and psychologism.

These elements required for the elaboration of a theory of
ideology reveal at last the importance of the category of the *subject:* a particularly intricate and enigmatic category in Althusser's
approach to psychoanalysis considered as a key to understanding
the ideological humanization process, identified as the subjectivization process.

In that respect, we should pay particular attention to the end of the second talk, which propounds a study of the Cartesian *cogito* together with the genealogy of the institution of the subject as a main category of idealist philosophy. This genealogical inquiry uses the opposition between Spinozism and Cartesianism with respect to the philosophical category of a "subject of truth," a "subject of objectivity": a subject of knowledge identified as the Cartesian *cogito*, which was remarkably rejected in Spinoza's philosophy, as is shown by Althusser's analysis of "Spinoza's abandonment of the subject of objectivity."

What is to be noted at this stage is the relation sketched out, through Althusser's genealogy of the *cogito,* between the institution of the subject in philosophy and the elaboration of the *psychological subject.*

Here, the Cartesian subject of truth and knowledge, the philosophical subject, appears to be implied by a whole theory of knowledge identified with a theory of judgment: the jurisdiction of a philosophical subject endowed with the faculty of *deciding* the truth value of its own ideas. And this Cartesian view is opposed to Spinoza's conception of knowledge as a *production*, a "process without a subject," already theorized in *On the Improvement of the Understanding.*

More precisely, Descartes' perspective is seen as "a problematics that opposes truth to error." And this miscomprehension of the nature of the distinction between true and false lies exactly at the foundation of the philosophical institution of the subject—if one follows Althusser's provocative and rather elliptical hypothesis on that point. For him, the Cartesian problematics misunderstood the true meaning of the distinction or de-cision between truth and error. This is a philosophy of judgment, which "leads to a philosophy of the subject that decides between truth and error."

On the contrary, Althusser sees the break or distinction between true and false as having been adequately grasped by Spinoza in the framework of his unprecedented model of the mind, based on the rejection of the Cartesian theory of knowledge and certainty, that is, on the refusal of the distinction between will and intellect. This issue is at stake in Spinoza's abandonment of a subject of judgment, linked with an original conceptualization of truth independent of any "subject of truth," as shown by the crucial notion of *verum index sui et falsi* in the *On the Improvement of the Understanding* or the concept of *veritas norma sui et falsi* in the second part of the *Ethics*. This conceptualization forestalls the classical identification of the distinction between true and false with an external opposition and consequently refutes the postulate of a philosophical subject at the origin of this opposition.

Finally, at the end of the second talk the genealogy of the psychological subject, considered as the obscure duplicate of the subject of truth and objectivity in Descartes' *Meditations on First Philosophy*, is particularly interesting. The psychological subject, if it may be identified in Descartes' view as the subject of *error*, is the obscure correlate of the philosophical subject.

What Althusser sketches out in these last pages of the second talk is an archeology of the psychological subject critically understood as the pathological double of the philosophical Cartesian subject.

In conclusion, let us briefly underline the ambivalence inherent in Althusser's enigmatic philosophical treatment of the category of subject. On the one hand, the subject is a fundamental notion as regards Althusser's previously discussed theory of ideology. But, on the other hand, Althusser's critical reading of the philosophical subject considered as the theoretical premise for the elaboration of the psychological subject reveals a strong divergence with respect to Lacan in the interpretation of the Cartesian subject itself.

According to Lacan, the Cartesian subject, far from being a historical idealist category that constitutes the philosophical precondition of the psychological ego, should be understood on the contrary as an *empty subject*, the subject of science, which anticipates the Freudian subject: namely the subject of the unconscious as opposed to the psychological ego.[12] Althusser, whose thought was constantly marked by Spinoza's philosophy, could not accept such a rehabilitation of the Cartesian subject. His own reconstruction of the birth of the psychological subject remains dependent on an identification—contestable—of the *cogito* with the subject of consciousness: an identification that was consistently refuted by Lacan. This question of the subject represents the point where Althusser (who is in general so deeply indebted to Lacan's thought—and this is one of the main lessons of these two talks) departs from the initiator of the "return to Freud."

Yet, beyond these discordances, Althusser's strategic choice to grasp the forthcoming scientificity the human sciences through the particular prism of psychoanalysis must be explained by the *antipsychologistic claim at work in Freud's discovery* as it was revealed by Lacan. Thus it is shown that the human sciences, if they tend to scientificity, must break with behaviorism, anthropologism, psychology, and also with an idealist philosophy of the Subject, a philosophy of consciousness: just as psychoanalysis did, at the price of a continued effort.

We may then infer that the sole "real sciences" would be linguistics and psychoanalysis itself—once the latter has fully separated itself from its ideological background. A similar conception of what could be the emerging break between the human sciences and anthropologism, historical continuism, and psychologism can also be found a few years later in Foucault's *The Order of Things* (1966). In the framework of his archeological sequence, Foucault takes ethnology, linguistics, *and psychoanalysis* to be the models for such a liberation. The end of *The Order of Things* is, in that respect, quite remarkable and consonant with Althusser's earlier program of critically rethinking the scientific status of the human sciences, which already implied the delimitation of a "break" between *pseudo-sciences* (whose typical expression is psychology) and *real sciences* such as linguistics and, more laboriously, psychoanalysis itself.[13]

Editors' Preface

Olivier Corpet and François Matheron

THE TWO lectures published in this volume were delivered by Louis Althusser in the course of the seminar on Lacan and psychoanalysis held at the École normale supérieure during the academic year 1963–1964. This was the third seminar Althusser organized: after one on the young Marx held in 1961–1962 and another on the origins of structuralism held in 1962–1963; the one held the following year on Marx's *Capital* led to the publication of *Lire Le Capital.* At the same time, Althusser invited Lacan, who had been expelled from the Sainte-Anne Hospital, to set up his own seminar at the École normale supérieure, and its first session took place on January 15, 1964.[1] On December 6, 1963, Althusser also gave a long speech presenting the seminar of Pierre Bourdieu and Jean-Claude Passeron.[2] The time had come, he thought, to make strategic alliances with the aim of changing the state of the theoretical field, which was then broadly dominated by "structuralist" problematics and more generally marked by the emergence of the "human sciences." In fact, with the almost simultaneous publication of *Pour Marx* and *Lire Le Capital* at the end of 1965, Althusser was rapidly to become a major theoretical authority for his period.

When Althusser organized his seminar on Lacan and psychoanalysis, he had already published most of the articles that were to be included in *Pour Marx;* on the other hand, he had so far written hardly anything on psychoanalysis, and it was precisely in the context of this seminar that he wrote, in early 1964, most of his article "Freud et Lacan."[3] However, these two lectures, far from being simple drafts of this famous work, have an incontestable originality. The accent is put on a question that is not central in "Freud et Lacan": "What place does psychoanalysis have today in the domain of the human sciences"? Which implies, Althusser immediately adds, "that we know very precisely what psychoanalysis itself is, and that we know very precisely what the general domain of the human sciences is." Whence immediately results a doubling of the inquiry; it involves both a question of fact and a question of right.

The question of fact: "today in 1963," in France, what "empirically factual" place does psychoanalysis occupy in the domain of the human sciences? This question can itself be answered only by making a long empirical detour through the history of the reception of psychoanalysis in France, which constitutes most of the first presentation. While taking care to explain that he proceeds in this way "for a provisional reason that," he hopes, "will soon be transcended," he nonetheless makes a proposal concerning which the least one can say is that it is hardly frequent in the work published during his lifetime: "I am going to tell you the story of my own encounter with this problem."

Question of right: "What must the relation between psychoanalysis and the domain of the human sciences be?" Althusser recognizes at the outset that this is question is no doubt "excessive," because the objective is simply "to define the theoretical conditions of the possibility of valid research in both the domain of psychoanalysis and the domain of the human sciences in general." The second presentation has as its goal to take up one of the aspects of this vast problem: that of the relations between psychoanalysis and psychology. By drawing a line of rigorous demarcation between these two disciplines, Althusser may have helped make his enterprise a little less excessive. When she arrives at the end of this volume, the reader will no doubt have a more precise idea of the peculiarly Althusserian interpretation of a position so characteristic of a period: the rejection of psychology.

The seminar of 1963–1964 on Lacan and psychoanalysis took place in the following way. The first presentation was that of Michel Tort, which was divided into three sessions and devoted to the general establishment of Freud's and Lacan's concepts. Althusser's first presentation was delivered between the first two sessions with Michel Tort. Étienne Balibar then devoted two sessions to talking about psychosis. Then came Jacques-Alain Miller's presentation on Lacan (three sessions). Achille Chiesa spoke next about Maurice Merleau-Ponty and psychoanalysis, then Yves Duroux spoke about "Psychoanalysis and Phenomenology." Then Althusser gave his second presentation, and the last speaker was Jean Mosconi ("Psychoanalysis and Anthropology").[4] Althusser's correspondence shows that he seriously considered publishing all these presentations, but the project was never realized.

Althusser's archives contain no written version of his presentations, or even the slightest collection of preparatory notes, and the recording of his second presentation clearly shows that he was not, on that day, reading a text written in advance, in contrast to what he did, for example, during the seminar on Marx's *Capital.* The text of the first presentation was established on the basis of the rough transcript (preserved in Althusser's archives) of a recording that has now disappeared: a transcript that is often very defective, especially with regard to proper names. In order to establish this text, we have therefore relied on the notes taken by Étienne Balibar, which were extremely valuable to us. The text of the second presentation was established on the basis of the transcription of a tape recording preserved in Althusser's archives, occasionally supplemented by Étienne Balibar's notes.

In both cases, we had a twofold goal: maintaining the specific rhetoric of the presentations and producing a legible text. This led us to make the following decisions: we simply omitted, without systematic indications, repetitions whose sole effect would have been to make the text syntactically incorrect; and we have also omitted, but indicating the suppressions by ellipses, incomplete sentences whose meaning could not be determined

(Althusser having interrupted himself in the middle of a sentence to begin another one); we modified certain sentences that were syntactically inadmissible, when their meaning was not in doubt; and finally we let stand certain sentences that were syntactically vague, when they seemed not to hinder reading. Naturally, we take complete responsibility for any errors of transcription that may have been made.

We would like to thank François Boddaert, Louis Althusser's heir, who has generously granted us his confidence, as well as Élisabeth Roudinesco and Étienne Balibar, without whom the establishment of the text of these presentations might have been an impossible task.

Psychoanalysis and
the Human Sciences

—

1

The Place of Psychoanalysis in the Human Sciences

THROUGH AN interpretation of Lacan, we shall seek to determine the place of psychoanalysis in the human sciences today, in 1963. There are two fundamental preconditions for this determination: 1. that we know precisely what psychoanalysis is and 2. that we know precisely what the general domain of the human sciences is. Consequently, this determination depends on: 1. an observation de facto: empirically, what place does psychoanalysis currently occupy, what is its practical role today, in the human sciences? 2. a question de jure: given the essence of psychoanalysis on the one hand and that of the human sciences on the other, what is the proper relation between the two? If today we can give an answer to this question de jure—an ambition that might obviously be considered excessive, as I would be the first to grant—in that very way we shall succeed in defining a field of research in which all theoretical, scientific, methodical, and rigorous reflection must necessarily enter insofar as it concerns either psychoanalysis itself or the domain of the human sciences.

The excessive enterprise involved in the series of presentations we are undertaking here is to precisely define the theoretical conditions of the possibility of valid research in the domains of both psychoanalysis and the human sciences in general. To that end I shall raise the problem in a somewhat unusual way by telling you right away that it can be raised in two different ways. First, in a perfectly objective way, abstracting from the speaker's personal experience; I could deal with the question without making any reference to my personal experience. However, I am going to proceed in another way, by recounting the story of my own encounter with this problem. This is not at all about me; I think everyone has had more or less the same experience, and that we encounter this problem through its practical manifestations, through a whole series of indexes. And, up to this point, the encounter has necessarily been a personal one. I emphasize its personal nature because there is no theory of this encounter, and because the definition of psychoanalysis, on the one hand, and that of the human sciences, on the other, as they currently exist has not given rise to a theoretical reflection that makes it possible to abstract from the concrete encounter with the problem experienced by each of us. It is solely for this reason—and thus for a historically provisional reason, which I hope will soon be transcended—that it is indispensable to show how this problem can be encountered by someone, given that currently the only way of encountering it is through a personal encounter, quite simply because it is not the subject of reflection. As a result, the problem is encountered in the experience of each person. Therefore I am going to tell you the story of my own encounter with this problem. Not a personal story, in the sense of individual, but personal in the intellectual sense of the term, including its problems.

Abstracting from all historical and autobiographical elements, I shall say simply this: for me, and I think for you as well, the encounter with psychoanalysis took place through the encounter with Freud's work. Obviously, psychoanalysis is found everywhere: in the media, on the street, etc., but in fact, from a theoretical point of view, that's not how it happens: at a certain point, we're going to examine Freud's texts. Then we are immediately confronted with a very serious, very profound obstacle of which Freud was perfectly well aware, which is represented by what Freud himself called the psychological resistance that is opposed to the admission of the very enterprise of psychoanalysis into the realm of public opinion. You know that Freud's earliest works met with an absolutely extraordinary barrage of criticism. Though psychoanalysis is now a recognized part of our cultural world, when Freud wrote his first works he was condemned by everyone. You know that the first person in France who had the courage to talk about Freud was Hesnard,[1] who thereby deserves our historical gratitude. He is still alive. He has published a book for which Merleau-Ponty wrote a preface before his death, and in France it was actually he who, I should say, did not introduce but rather pointed out Freud's existence, noting that a certain

Freud from Vienna who had worked in France, and what's more with Charcot, existed, and that he thought a certain number of things that might be of great importance. Freud was aware of this extraordinary resistance; he referred to it in his works, saying: what I say will not be well-received, and he offered an explanation for this. An explanation that, in my opinion, is historically false but was the only one he could give at that time. It's a psychoanalytic explanation and it goes as follows: My works will not be accepted because they put in question the psychic equilibrium of each individual who reads them, that is, his system of defense against his own neuroses. In other words, the concept of neurosis that Freud used to explain the resistance with which his works necessarily met was an analytical concept, but one that could not be thought de jure (if I may say so) in terms of the analytical concept invoked. And that is why Freud, having clearly sensed the theoretical difficulty involved in his explanation, subsequently produced another concept: that of the neurotic character of our civilization. In other words, Freud moved on to a genuinely historical explanation, but in terms of his analytical theory, that is, in terms of a practice that in principle addressed individuals. By proposing this second notion—our civilization is neurotic—Freud was offering a historical explanation for the inevitable resistance with which his theory collided in its very diffusion. But in doing so he modified the historical status of the concept of neurosis. And he supposed that our culture, as such, was neurotic, that is, that a historical subject—no longer an individual, but a historical culture—could be the object, or rather the seat, of a pathological affection of the neurotic type. Thus he raised a problem that was no longer psychoanalytic in nature but rather historical. He formulated the consequent difficulty this way: the theory I propose meets with an extremely deep ideological resistance, which may have certain affinities with the structures of psychoanalytic resistance that I find in individuals, but in fact cannot be reduced to those structures because the object is not the same. This is not a matter of an individual, Freud, explaining his theory to a neurotic individual (the resistance being explained by the individual's neurosis), but of Freud explaining to whole masses of people, including scientists, an enterprise that was scientific in spirit and collided with a resistance that he attributed to the general resistance of our civilization, that is, with a resistance that was no longer psychological, no longer psychoanalytic, but ideological and historical. Despite the current prejudice favorable to psychoanalysis, and even though our civilization's general attitude to Freud has changed, we still encounter this difficulty when we read Freud's texts—but for us it has taken a different form that I shall now proceed to define.

For us, this resistance took a very precise form: that of the inadequation between the concepts that Freud uses in his texts and the content that these concepts are intended to grasp. This inadequation can be expressed this way: the concepts Freud proposes are imported concepts, in the Kantian sense. You know that Kant contrasts the concepts a science has produced by itself in the course of its own development, which belong to it organically, to concepts he terms "imported," namely concepts that a science uses, that it needs, that it necessarily needs to use, but that it has not itself produced in its organic development, that it has borrowed from scientific disciplines existing outside it. This is exactly Freud's case. Freud set forth this analytical theory using imported concepts that were borrowed from biology, from the theory of energy in physics, and from political economy. That is, from three domains, three disciplines, that were then giving rise to a historically dated scientific elaboration: the then dominant biological theory, more or less inspired by Darwin; the theory of energy in physics, which was also dominant; and, finally, economic theory (an allusion to the possibility of a knowledge of the economic world and economic laws), all of which it was possible to think and could be used in their conceptual forms within another domain.

There we have the true difficulty that we encounter, even today, when we read Freud's texts: we wonder what relation there can be between what Freud designates by his concepts and the theoretical status of concepts that are obviously borrowed, and which, in any event, needed, in order to become domestic concepts, to be profoundly transformed, that is, needed to undergo a theoretical transformation following a theoretical reflection. Now we have to note that until Lacan appeared this theoretical transformation following a theoretical reflection did not take place.

Until Lacan appeared—that is, until an attempt to transform imported concepts into domestic concepts—every reader of Freud encountered a contradiction between Freud's concepts and the concrete content of what he calls psychoanalysis.

The question I am now asking is the following: what does psychoanalysis designate by these concepts, which have, up to now, not been examined theoretically and have not been transformed from imported concepts into domestic concepts? Everyone agrees to the reality these imported concepts of Freud's designate: it is the practice of analysis itself. That is why, when we encounter psychoanalysis, we all agree that something is going on in it. Not that it's only a technique of readaptation, liberation, etc.: it's a technique that is situated within a practice. I don't want to use the term *praxis,* which would introduce us to a general theory—which I would gladly use; let us say that psychoanalysis is a praxis situated in the domain of praxis in general, etc.[2] Let's leave that aside, because it's a philosophical theorization that assumes the theoretical question of the precise status of the object concerned is already settled and perhaps reflected. This is not the case. But everyone will recognize that what Freud's psychoanalytic concepts designate, not in their domestic but in their imported form, is a real practice, that is, the fact that Freud is dealing with patients whom he treats in a practice that is called therapy.

So at this point we are referred to therapy itself. When we encounter psychoanalysis, after having struggled with the theoretical difficulties I've mentioned, and after having noted, consequently, that the theoretical concept can't provide us with access to the thing itself, we're obliged to say that the thing itself is located in the actual practice of psychoanalytic technique, that is, in therapy. And this is where we find ourselves at a real dead end. Why? Because everyone—including especially psychoanalysts themselves, and first of all everyone who has been through analysis, will tell you that psychoanalytic treatment gives rise to an experience of therapy, to a specific and irreducible experience. Psychoanalysts and their patients can be, to some extent, compared to soldiers who explain that a civilian can't understand anything about the army without having performed his military service. You have to have been through that. In the language of the psychoanalysts and their patients, this takes the following form: you have to do it live. That is, you have to go through the concrete experience of therapy and the institutional reality of the necessity of this direct, irreducible experience of therapy; that is didactic analysis. In other words, psychoanalysis has created an institution, without which no one can gain access to his own truth, and calls it didactic psychoanalysis: it requires every psychoanalyst to personally undergo the concrete experience of the analytic situation and posits as an absolute principle an effect that is not made an object of reflection de jure, but is affirmed de facto, gives rise to an institution, and in fact selects the psychoanalysts themselves. De facto, it went beyond this principle in the form of an institution that was called didactic psychoanalysis, which is itself subject to a whole body, that is, no one can become a psychoanalyst without being certified by the existing psychoanalytic societies, but no one can be certified without having undergone a didactic psychoanalysis, and no one can undergo a didactic psychoanalysis without having received authorization to undergo the didactic psychoanalysis in question with psychoanalysts who have been designated by the existing psychoanalytic society as suitable for undergoing a didactic psychoanalysis. Notice to what extent, in the facts themselves, in the practice itself and in the institutions—not of the world outside psychoanalysis but of psychoanalysis itself—what each of us can experience in his encounters or conversations with either an analyst or with an analysand is sanctioned in the following way: you have to have gone through that, you have to have done it live, because it's an absolutely irreducible concrete experience. You can't understand from outside what you have to have lived through in order to know what it's about.

But here we find ourselves confronted by another difficulty: the analysts and the analysands, for their part, have met this requirement. They have actually gone through it, they've done it live, they've lived through the specifics of this situation and they're trying to express it. You will find quite a few things in books and in texts with theoretical pretensions written by psychoanalysts in which they try to conceive what is specific to this situation. We will see later how they manage it—how they think they manage it. But the fact is that both anecdotal expression (we're telling the psychoanalysts' story) and attempts at theoretical expression of the necessity of passing through the concrete experience of this irreducible practice known as psychoanalytic therapy lead to the absolutely stupefying paradox that all that has never convinced anyone. This is because all the descriptions of therapy, all the reflections on therapy that currently exist, are absolutely incapable of taking the place of theoretical concepts that would actually make it possible to have access not only to what analytic practice is—which is only part of what is involved—but to that of which it is the concrete substance, namely its own theory. In other words, there is no satisfactory psychoanalytic theory that reflects on the reality of psychoanalysis, the status of the psychoanalyst, the scientific status of psychoanalytic practice; there is no satisfactory scientific theory that could be reduced to a theory of therapy. Nothing we're told about therapy ever succeeds in reaching the point where a theory of therapy could be transformed into a theory of psychoanalysis itself. That means that everything we're told about therapy never manages to transform a theorization of analytic practice into a theory of psychoanalysis itself.

On the other hand, this sheds light on another very important phenomenon, which is our third way of encountering psychoanalysis concretely. I remind you of the first two: Freud's own texts, with the difficulties they contain, namely the inadequation between the concepts and their content and the psychoanalytic practice itself and its inability to produce a theory of psychoanalysis. We encounter psychoanalysis in a third way in contemporary philosophy. We have to talk about France, because this cultural universe is very deeply marked, not only so far as philosophy is concerned but also in all the cultural disciplines, by this absolutely extraordinary characteristic that is commonly found in Italy: provincialism. By that I mean that since the end of the eighteenth century one of the fundamental traits of French culture in all its domains has been an incredible ignorance of what is going on elsewhere, what is going on in other countries. When Italians call themselves provincialists, they mean: we are a country that has not succeeded in establishing its national unity, all our cities are only provincial capitals; our national unity is recent—Rome is our capital, but it is an arbitrary administrative capital; everything happens outside us, everything happens in Europe. And the great aspiration of Italian culture is to rise to the European level. But before Italian economic production reaches the European level, we can say that Italians truly experienced the nostalgia of not being at the European cultural level. And they experienced it in a concrete manner, as we can see: the country in the world that publishes the most translations of works written in foreign languages is Italy. And today the country in the world in which the fewest works are translated from foreign languages is France. . . . I simply want to say that I'm forced to speak about the French ideological situation, about the French cultural situation, so far as philosophy is concerned, and that's why I've taken this personal example, because it has a historical meaning. Concretely, we encounter psychoanalysis in philosophy; we encounter it in a number of extremely precise, extremely concrete philosophies. I am going to say a word about them.

I'm not talking about Dalbiez. He's interesting, of course, historically interesting. His enormous two-volume work on psychoanalysis has just been reprinted.[3] I think it never taught anyone anything, that it was a behaviorist attempt to present psychoanalysis; it is a phenomenon that is theoretically obsolete. I'm not talking about Hesnard, who played the historical role of presenting psychoanalysis in France, and whose book had a preface written by Merleau-Ponty. But the fact that the man who presented psychoanalysis in France, the historical initiator of psychoanalysis in France, published a work for which Merleau-Ponty wrote a preface is extremely interesting because, so far as I'm concerned, philosophy's encounter with psychoanalysis passed, in France, through Sartre and Merleau-Ponty. And this encounter that we make in Sartre and Merleau-Ponty—if we're lucky enough to get our hands on this work, which has never been reprinted and practically disappeared from libraries—has its origin in Politzer.[4] It was through Politzer that it began; it was through Politzer that psychoanalysis became an object of philosophical reflection. And it was through Politzer that psychoanalysis entered into French philosophical reflection, expressly and without any doubt, in the work of Sartre and Merleau-Ponty.

In a little while I'll tell you how things looked in that respect—I'm still talking about my personal experience. I want to say that I also encountered psychoanalysis in the work of Sartre and Merleau-Ponty and I was lucky enough to get my hands on Politzer, and I read him. Obviously, there was somebody named Lacan, absolutely unintelligible. . . . But from now on I'm going to tell you what form my little personal synthesis took and what form it retained until, let's say, about two or three years ago. The form taken by my little personal synthesis, that is, my personal attempt to respond to this problem, which is not solely a theoretical problem but a real problem (it is encountered in life, it raises concrete problems, etc., including even practical problems: when a guy is sick, can he work?).

There are currently two psychoanalytic societies in France. The society that Lacan founded in a schism that dates from 1953 and the old one, presided over by Nacht.[5] There are violent conflicts that can have repercussions on the technique, that is, on the healing one can expect from one psychoanalyst or another. Apart from individual abilities, the two societies pursue very different general lines of argument. It might thus be thought (at least by those of us who believe that a theory never remains without consequences, always has practical effects) that it could also produce differences in the technique of therapy (that is also what Lacan says all the time) and even in the results that can be expected from it. Now I'm going to explain to you the little personal synthesis I arrived at. And in so doing we will encounter another reality—not only psychoanalysis but also the human sciences.

I'd arrived at the following little synthesis whose ultimate principles were Politzer's theoretical bases, which were also found in Sartre and Merleau-Ponty. I was a little prejudiced, for different reasons, against Sartre's and Merleau-Ponty's philosophical syntheses, so I had a tendency to return to Politzer, telling myself: let's go back to the sources; at least the water will be pure.

What was the result? Politzer was the man who had said psychology doesn't exist, psychology is the theory of the soul. Why doesn't psychology exist? Because, on the one hand, it's a science that claims to have as its object the soul, that is, an object that doesn't exist and, on the other hand, because it's a discipline that uses concepts that are only abstractions. Neither its object nor its concepts exist. The abstractions of classical psychology are concepts of the faculties of the soul: they don't exist, and that's completely to be expected, since the object that classical psychology studies is the soul, and the soul doesn't exist. So we're going to create [a psychology without a soul], and that's how Politzer heralded the advent of a new epoch. His text is a genuine manifesto: now it is beginning. That is the meaning of his *Critique des fondements de la psychologie*. You have to read it, because it's fundamental for the culture of our time. . . . What is beginning is exactly the opposite of what existed earlier. Instead of dealing with a psychology whose object was the soul, we are dealing with a psychology without a soul; on the other hand, we're going to create a psychology that instead of having abstract concepts like the faculties of the soul, sensation, memory, etc., will have concrete concepts. That's the program. It's defined by Politzer on the basis of an existing reality, namely classical and critical psychology: this program is defined in purely negative terms. We are going to create a psychology without soul, we're agreed on that, but it has to have an object: that object will be the concrete; it will be drama. Classical psychology, Politzer said, is a psychology in the third person: we're going to create a first-person psychology. That's what concrete means. Classical psychology used abstract concepts, third-person concepts: we're going to use concrete concepts, concepts in the first person. There you have Politzer's mythical idea, which was the content of his program, which coincided with his program: psychology will never exist unless it is a concrete psychology. It became a fact, since Politzer tried to found a *Revue de psychologie concrète* that, I think . . . never came out.[6] It was impossible, because what Politzer was in fact designating, in relation to classical psychology, was what we call the nonconcept of classical psychology, that is, a domain of reality that is defined negatively on the basis of existing concepts but is not defined conceptually. And the proof is that when Politzer tried to define the concrete object he was dealing with, he simply uttered, reuttered indefinitely ad nauseam, the words *concrete, concrete, concrete,* the words *drama, drama, "drama,* the words *first person, first person, first person.*

These expressions might designate something, but in a negative way: it's not abstract; it's concrete; it's not a phenomenon that takes place outside concrete psychological life or the subject; it takes place within and it's dramatic, etc., but from a theoretical point of view, that is, from the conceptual point of view, it produced nothing; it could only indicate the domain that had to be explored and that didn't indicate the theoretical concepts that defined the domain on the basis of which theoretical research was possible. In other words, if we try to examine the theoretical status of the concepts by means of which Politzer designated this new object, we don't get anywhere. This is shown today in a few texts, a few articles, especially in the article by Laplanche that Tort cited last time.[7] What Politzer said, which was essential, is that the concrete—concrete psychology—is in psychoanalysis. He said, in short: [concrete psychology] exists but it doesn't know it,[8] I'm telling it that it exists, that is, I'm telling it that it exists in psychoanalysis. And, at the same time, Politzer said: unfortunately psychoanalysis is itself contaminated by classical psychology. Politzer said: for psychoanalysis, which is really concrete psychology without psychology knowing it, to be able to play its role as a theoretical guide in the domain of psychology, psychoanalysis itself has to be relieved of its heritage from classical psychology, namely the abstractions, its theory of the unconscious, as the *es,* the "id," as a reality interior to consciousness, as something irreducible, as another unconscious consciousness. In short, all of Freud's concepts have to go, including the concept of the complex; in other words, Politzer rejected all Freud's operative concepts on the pretext that they were abstract. From our point of view, that is an essential point: no reflection can take place without being able to use abstract concepts, and the problem is not played out between concepts that are abstract and others that are not, that is, nonconcepts, but between scientific abstract concepts and nonscientific abstract concepts. And the proof of this is that the concepts that Politzer proposed as concrete concepts to replace the concepts of classical psychology, which he declared to be abstract, or Freudian concepts that Freud had inherited from classical psychology, all those concrete concepts through which Politzer designated the concrete object of what was supposed to be psychoanalysis, on the one hand, and of what psychology was supposed to become through it, on the other hand, all these concepts are not theoretical concepts, that is, they have no valid scientific status that would make it possible to use them to work out a theory or undertake research. When Politzer said that the concepts had to be concrete, it's clear we can contrast the first chapter of Hegel's *Phenomenology of Mind* with him. The concept of the first person claims to be concrete, but it's an abstraction. Exactly as the "this" is an abstraction, a generality. The concept of drama, which claims to be concrete, is an abstract concept, a generality. And so far as we are concerned, we can say that we are simply at a theoretical dead-end: it's a bad abstraction because it doesn't go anywhere—anywhere other than to Merleau-Ponty and Sartre.

My personal synthesis took the following very precise form: psychology . . . which is in search of itself in the domain of human sciences, already exists, but psychology doesn't know it. Psychology was founded, and nobody noticed. It was founded by Freud. Thus all that is required for it to constitute itself is that present-day psychology become aware that its essence was defined by Freud and that it draw the consequences of that fact. . . . Thus it suffices to become aware of the fact that just as Galileo defined the essence of physics as such by saying physics as such is the physical capable of being measured, that is, he defined the essence of a region of the existent; and in the same way psychology can develop only on the condition that it become aware of the essence of the object that it has to develop; and the essence of the object that it has to develop, the essence of the psychic, is the unconscious. In other words, it took this amusing form: the object of psychology is the unconscious. Psychology can develop only by defining, by means of this essence, the object of psychology as the unconscious. I more or less adopted Politzer's criticism . . . which consisted in saying: basically, psychology up to now has drawn on the prejudice of the soul, and I said in another way: psychology has up to now drawn on the prejudice of the consciousness, it has not become aware of the fact that the essence of its object is the unconscious. In this way, in fact, I juxtaposed a certain encounter with psychology, with psychoanalysis itself, with another encounter that I was making, that we all make, which is the encounter of psychoanalysis with the social sciences themselves, that is, with an objective reality.

In this way I pass from what we might call the personal side, that is, the autobiographical and intellectual side of the exposition of the problem, to an objective exposition of the problem, which can be formulated as follows: what is the current status of psychoanalysis in relation to the human sciences and particularly in relation to psychology? The second part of my reflections, which I will also divide into two parts: the scientific relation of psychoanalysis to psychology, on the one hand, and the ideological relation of psychoanalysis to philosophy, on the other hand.

Let's turn first to the scientific relation of between psychoanalysis and psychology. The paradox of the present situation can be put this way: after having been rejected by the culture of his time, Freud was accepted; now he is everywhere; he has invaded. That raises a problem, but we can't reflect immediately on this problem. We can start from it to reflect on the question—which is what Lacan also does. In any case, the observation from which we have to start is that everywhere we see an absolutely profound symbiosis between psychoanalysis and psychology in the current state of the social sciences. And we see it on both sides; in other words, this encounter does not occur solely on the side of psychology: on the one hand, we see psychology reaching out to psychoanalysis and, on the other, we see psychoanalysis reaching out to psychology. These two things are happening at the same time, we can show that in a very precise way.

On the side of psychoanalysis, what is approaching psychology?[9] It's what Tort mentioned last time: all the developments of psychoanalysis concerning the development of the psychoanalysis of children. In Freud you have a series of texts: *Little Hans, Three Essays on Sexuality*; all that underwent considerable development. With Freud, generally speaking, a whole series of psychoanalysts who specialize in children, specialists who did not exist earlier, has developed, producing an extremely abundant literature. Psychoanalysis also approached psychology through a whole series of disciplines on the borders of psychoanalysis—I'll come back to this notion of borders later—in particular, psychiatry and psychosomatic medicine. In general, we can say that psychoanalysis revived psychiatry—that's incontestable. Nosological descriptions, that is, descriptions of the visible structures of illnesses, which constituted most of what psychiatry did, were overthrown and revived by psychoanalysis's intervention. The face of psychiatry has largely changed. Psychosomatic medicine, a discipline that did not exist before, was constituted as a kind of general medicine, treating, through psychotherapy, a certain number of ailments that can be identified only by using Freudian concepts, that is, a certain number of symptoms that do not fall into the domain of general or organic medicine, but rather of a psychotherapy. Similarly, we can also note that psychoanalysis approached social psychology insofar as it provided it with a whole series of concepts that are at work in all the most current developments in social psychology. Whether it's a matter of investigations into motivation, studies on advertising, etc., you find psychoanalytic concepts, and it seems that psychoanalysis took the initiative. Very specific names are associated with this: names of psychoanalysts who've done studies that could be listed here. I'll spare you the list.

One last, extremely important, point: psychoanalysis approached the general object of the human sciences by approaching anthropology. This is already found in Freud or at least apparently in Freud: *Totem and Taboo, Civilization and Its Discontents, The Future of an Illusion.* All these books deal with cultural phenomena, and thus anthropological phenomena, and they all present themselves as having the ambition to extend psychoanalytic concepts to the disciplines of anthropology and history that deal with cultural objects. You know that in America, in particular, this kind of research is currently undergoing considerable development. American anthropological studies, for example, the works of Margaret Mead, Kardiner,[10] et al., are usually written by people who have either been analyzed themselves or who have had psychoanalytic training. And all that came directly from psychoanalysis itself.

On the other hand (I'm not going to describe this from the other side), all these disciplines—child psychology, psychology, social psychology, psychiatry, etc.—have approached psychoanalysis as well, that is, they have gone in search of concepts they needed to account for phenomena that had previously escaped them. That has given rise to attempts that are sometimes extremely interesting but relatively isolated. For example, the attempt made by Spitz. Spitz is French, I think, or is of French origin, and currently lives in America.[11] He has published several works—two or three—and he's doing research aimed at constituting a psychoanalytic psychology of child development. He's trying to create an experimental psychology that psychoanalysis needs in order to encounter its own concepts in concrete form. In other words, what Spitz is seeking in the observation of children, and not in an analytical relation with the child, is direct observation of the oral stage, the anal stage, etc. That is, he's seeking in psychology the actual reality of psychoanalytic concepts themselves. I won't go into Melanie Klein and Anna Freud: all that belongs to the domain of child psychology: we're right in the middle of these border zones.

I'd like to mention another encounter between psychology and psychoanalysis that is extremely important and extremely typical,. In short, the encounter that has taken place up to now has been one between psychoanalysis and a psychology without any genuine biological or psychosocial foundation. But an extremely interesting encounter that we can call indirect is taking place on another terrain: that of psychophysiology and biology. This terrain is obviously the most interesting, for the following reason: biology exists as a science; in any case it is a scientific discipline that has scientific qualifications. So does psychophysiology. The clearest example is Wallon. Wallon developed a psychology that is original with respect to classical psychology, and it is heavily used, especially by Marxists who take an interest in these problems. Wallon developed a psychology that can be considered, formally, in contrast to classical psychology, a dialectical psychology. . . . Everything that is dialectical being Marxist, or rather nothing that is dialectical being foreign to Marxism (according to an adage that ought to be written in Latin to give it all its power), everything that is dialectical is ours. Wallon being dialectical, he's necessarily a Marxist. On what is this assimilation based? It's based on the concept of stage. Wallon, drawing on the works of neurologists who have, in fact, identified biological, neurological, etc. stages of psychological maturation, has shown a kind of parallel between the existence of stages of biological, neurological, etc., maturation, on the one hand, and the existence of stages of psychological maturation, on the other hand. He has established a parallel and a correspondence between them, that is, he has observed, in fact, that the essential stages coincide. And among other things, an amusing detail: he is the first to have emphasized the fundamental importance of the "mirror stage," a fact that Lacan—I wouldn't say has never pardoned him, but in any case has always managed to avoid mentioning.[12] Because it also happens that psychoanalysts sometimes read texts that are not purely psychoanalytic or psychiatric. When it happened that someone said, to Lacan, but your mirror stage was already in Wallon, he flew into one of those historic rages that, if they had received the public notice they should have, would have shaken at least the Arc de Triomphe.

What matters in all this is that, in actuality, another encounter between psychology and psychoanalysis becomes detectable. An encounter regarding the very structure of the type of development that appears in psychoanalysis, on the one hand, and in psychology, on the other. In psychoanalysis, as in psychology, it seems that we are dealing with a dialectical development in stages, and Wallon is the theoretician of this encounter. Even if he never talks about psychoanalysis, in fact, in his work there is— and this has been used by some theoreticians who claim to follow him, as soon as psychoanalytic concepts have been allowed to go into circulation—what is necessary to found a theoretical rapprochement between psychoanalysis and psychology....

The third encounter between psychology and psychoanalysis takes place on a third terrain: that of society itself. This is doubtless the most interesting point. Here I am only developing everything Tort said, and in particular when he described Lacan's critique of existing psychoanalysis as the critique of the psychoanalyses of social adaptation. It takes place on the terrain of society. This presupposes two convergent conditions for the encounter: on the side of psychoanalysis and on that of sociology.[13] Let's look first at the side of psychoanalysis. This is based on a theoretical interpretation of what Freud calls the reality principle. I don't want to give a detailed history of this subject—that could be done, and it's very important—but here's the gist of it: the reality principle has gradually come to be interpreted as representing the reality of society, that is, the object of psychoanalysis has been interpreted as the resultant of the interaction between the child as a biological being and the social milieu in which he lives, and in which he receives his life in the first moment, and at the same time as his life, the norms of his upbringing, that is, the social constraints society teaches him through the intermediary of his parents, and particularly his mother—constraints that take the form, first, of the regulation of nutrition, that is, the timing of the moments when the breast is offered to the child, second, toilet training, etc., and it goes on like that. The reality principle is society, not in its material reality, not in the fact of feeding the child, etc., but in the norms that the immediate familial entourage transmits to and imposes on the child, norms that are the necessary regulations of the society itself. Everything thus depends on the oedipal moment; this oedipal moment, which interests Sartre in particular, is supposed to be the moment when the child interiorizes the reality principle, that is, assumes the obligations that are imposed on him by society, that is, no longer wets his diaper, to take a symbolic example, simply because he knows that he must no longer do that. He knows it, and that is the "superego." That's a particular example. In short, the fundamental authority that is going to dominate the child's life from this moment on explains his whole development: the superego that controls the setting up of all the other subordinate agencies is simply a specific moment that can, moreover, be considered the moment when neurological maturation, motor maturation, visual maturation, biological maturation, and psychological maturation converge, and it happens to be precisely the moment when the child interiorizes the social obligation that is imposed on him in exchange for life and the forms that that social obligation takes. Now, this is very important, first of all because it determines a whole interpretation of the meaning of psychoanalysis, and then of its practice, and also a whole, very amusing theoretical reflection on psychoanalysis itself. If, in fact, the object of psychoanalysis, in this case, is the product of the interaction of the individual and the social milieu, if the object of psychoanalysis has to be examined, first, on the basis of the individual's biological drives and, second, on that of social constraints imposed on the individual through the mediation of the proximate environment (of the father and the mother, and particularly the mother, over whom looms, moreover, the superior authority of the father who gives her his name, food, orders, who organizes the house, who protects her from the outside, who is a legal person with a legal situation determined in society): if everything happens there, to know what psychoanalysis is as an object, we have to be able, first, to make use of biology and the science of society. But—and this is an extremely important consequence—this means that we can really find the object of psychoanalysis in society. If you read Sartre's interpretations . . . you'll see that this is the nodal point, because it's where praxis, the individual project, is integrated into society. I would even say that it's Sartre's pineal gland, that is, the infinitesimal point of encounter, as small as possible, absolutely unassignable—but, after all, there has to be a meeting point somewhere. It's simply here that we find it, exactly as for Descartes, near the pineal gland.[14] It's in this region—we define a region where there is a point of coincidence—that this takes place; it's there that the individual project becomes social praxis, is accepted as such, etc.

This has significant practical consequences. They exist in broad daylight; they're obvious in all of what Lacan calls "American psychoanalysis," which is a veritable psychoanalysis of adaptation to the social milieu; that is, it's the exact opposite of psychoanalysis. If, in fact, the reality principle is only an intervention made on the individual by social norms that operate through the mediation of the proximate family milieu and that are assumed by the individual himself in the form of the superego, then analytic therapy becomes simply a negotiation between the individual and society, a negotiation that, like all delicate negotiations, needs the good offices of the psychoanalyst who will fix things, and who will fix them, of course, by saying: this poor boy, society has been too much for him, he's been crushed by it, that is, his ego has been crushed by his superego. The ego was too weak; we're going to strengthen it: it's the whole psychoanalysis of the ego's defense systems, whose great theoretician is Anna Freud, who is one of Lacan's personal enemies—well, not personal, but theoretically personal enemies—to whom he has never given the title that for him is the certification not of theoretical consciousness but of the presence of theory in her theoretical unconsciousness: the title of "brilliant tripe butcher" (*tripière géniale*). He gives that title to Melanie Klein.[15] And he calls Françoise Dolto a tripe butcher. This qualification, which exists only in the feminine form, is interesting: she's not brilliant yet, but she might become brilliant. In any case, Anna Freud is neither brilliant nor, a fortiori, a tripe butcher, because one can say brilliant only in connection with the title of tripe butcher: she's not even a tripe butcher; she just sells meat covered with cellophane. And the meat sold by Anna Freud is quite simply what you can buy under the cellophane covers of the Presses Universitaires de France, namely the work entitled *Mécanisme de défense du moi* or another work entitled *La Psychanalyse des enfants*.[16] In these works you see presented her little theory, in the form of analytical concepts strengthened—we'll see why in a moment—by a strong dose of castrating obsessions; this official psychoanalyst, being Freud's daughter, felt the need to become the archetypal psychoanalytic mother of a family, of the world of psychoanalysis . . . and she is received as such by the world of analytic culture. All this, obviously, without talking about society. But there are people who, dare I say, lack these scruples and speak openly about society: the whole current of American psychoanalysis, etc., and the techniques to which it gives rise. The representative of this trend, one of its representatives, even though he has a very strong Freudian culture, is Alexander.[17] . . . If someday you glance at one of Alexander's books—there are worse; we can consider him a good witness, he's a guy who has a good Freudian culture—you will often find these matters explained, popularized in concrete institutions; they don't remain at the stage of speculations. I don't know if you have ever read the fifth and sixth pages of *Le Monde*—I don't know what *Le Monde's* ulterior motive for publishing these things is (maybe it's malicious—I hope so—and I have a hard time seeing how they could be published without malice), for publishing reviews of an institution that is currently undergoing a very extensive development, but I hasten to tell you that it is not the only such institution, because there are many of them, in France and even in Paris, but let's say that it's the most famous, and, in any case, the one that is established, to which *Le Monde's* special correspondent can go and which has its offices at Jouy-en-Josas and provides training to the managers of big industrial firms to help them liquidate psychological problems that may arise among the managers themselves and thus between the managers of a firm and its employees. The problem then becomes that of the readaptation to the immediate social milieu, and all these analytical techniques are used. . . .

Thus this has provided access to a whole series of techniques that actually exist, have been implemented, and represent the practical use of this theoretical conception of the reality principle, thus of the superego and thus of the object of psychoanalysis. Now, what interests us the most, after the theory, are the theoretical consequences of the thing. Starting from the moment people realized that the reality principle, that is, the fundamental object of psychoanalysis, is to be sought in the direction of society, we saw the rise of psychoanalytic theories that are anthropological in character and that tried to relativize psychoanalysis itself, and its concepts themselves, on the basis of the preceding theoretical observation. We found ourselves confronted by psychoanalytic attempts that explained the following to us: psychoanalytic concepts are connected with a psychoanalytic object whose origin is to be sought in the relations between a biological being (the little child) and a specific society, and the superego, the establishment of authorities, represents the interiorization of the norms of social constraint in that society and its structure. So if we're dealing with Freud's concepts, that is, because he was Viennese, because he lived in a Western society, which is a patriarchal society, with a family structured in a historically determined way, imposing on the individuals who compose it a certain number of legal rules that reflect the economic-political-social structure of the society, and that find their realization in the immediate entourage, to the point that the pineal gland takes the form of the family as we know it. But there are societies that do not know this kind of family because there's a pineal gland different from our own: so let's develop a theory of other pineal glands, that is, a general theory of the possibility as such of forms of concrete variations on the Western pineal gland. And that gives us Malinowski, it gives us a whole trend in the American psychoanalytic enterprise according to which each society has, I would say, the complexes it deserves, the psychoanalysts it deserves, etc.

That can serve to introduce us to the understanding of what there is to be understood in theory of the shaman proposed by Lévi-Strauss, who is becoming a specialist in generalizing the pineal gland, because it is itself his object. He tells us that the shaman of a primitive society is the same thing as the psychoanalyst, that society gives the psychoanalyst the same mission as primitive society gives the shaman: liquidating symbolically the society's conflicts with itself by administering therapy to an individual declared by society to be mad or sick. If you study—and please do that—the chapter of Lévi-Strauss's *Anthropologie structurale* on the theory of the shaman, you will immediately see what space this reflection moves in.

There you have the domains in which psychoanalysis and psychology meet, those in which psychoanalysis and biology meet, [and finally] those in which psychoanalysis and society meet, with their theoretical consequences and practices. In the current situation there is obviously another domain of encounter, and it is where psychoanalysis and philosophy meet or, rather, where a certain number of themes borrowed from psychoanalysis are exploited by existing philosophies. I said enough a while ago, talking about Politzer, not to need to return to this at length. What I want to say is simply that the three preceding encounters I indicated can be juridically, theoretically authorized by the possibility of using psychoanalytic concepts in psychology, sociology, and anthropology or by the possibility of using psychological, biological, neurological, or sociological concepts in psychoanalysis. In other words, the three kinds of encounter that I've analyzed up to this point occur at the level of concepts, that is, they are favors of a conceptual order done to psychoanalysis by other disciplines. There is no encounter without an exchange. What is exchanged between psychoanalysis and the other disciplines we've mentioned up to now is concepts . . .

What I'm going to say now does not concern concepts. What is going to be exchanged between psychoanalysis and philosophy is not concepts. I would say that it's the concrete sense. More exactly, the exchange will take place in the following manner: in general, psychoanalysis is going to give philosophy the concrete, and philosophy is going to give psychoanalysis concepts. This takes place in the following manner: philosophy is going to explain to psychoanalysis that, if it wants to conceive the concrete with which it deals in a therapeutic practice that is still theoretically blind, it has to borrow its concepts from philosophy. It's very interesting: it's a question of practice, whereas before it was a question of theoretical exchanges. . . . The exchange takes place like this: psychoanalysis gives philosophy the concrete, that is, practically, let's call a spade a spade, the dual situation of the relation between doctor and patient: this is the object that psychoanalysis gives to philosophy. And philosophy, in turn, is going to give psychoanalysis concepts for thinking about this thing that philosophy then considers as constituting the true object and essence of psychoanalysis itself. Exchange—fair's fair—means that in these two exchanges there is one partner who imposes his law: that is, philosophy, when it says [to psychoanalysis], "I'm going to define your status for you, and then it's settled, we won't talk about it any more." That's Sartre's and Merleau-Ponty's discourse, following Politzer's discourse. This "it's settled, we won't talk about it any more" is the philosophical concept in which the realities of the psychoanalytic experience of therapy are developed. And this reality of the psychoanalytic experience is essentially the relation between the doctor and the patient. This is also a fundamental point in Lacan's reflection. It's a fundamental point for explaining, for saying: here's what's actually happening, that is, for demonstrating that the philosophical interpretation of the doctor-patient relationship is a theoretical imposture, for demonstrating that philosophy, in order to be able to digest this reality philosophically, has to falsify it. That's Lacan's basic demonstration regarding psychotherapy. Philosophy has to falsify the experience of reality, of the analytical practice itself, in order to be able to declare it to be philosophical. How is this theoretical imposture carried out? (It's just an expression; I apologize for its violence, but it's a purely theoretical violence.) Through the following postulate: what is at stake in the doctor-patient relationship, in the dual relationship of psychotherapy, is very simply the *pour autrui* ("for others"), it is very simply intersubjectivity, that is, the fundamental concept of what we might call the existentialist, personalist current that is one of the great trends of the present period and that flows through countless mouths from the springs of modern history. Obviously, Politzer's role in this context was absolutely decisive, because it was he who provided these concepts. When Politzer contrasted third-person knowledge with first-person knowledge, when he explained that this took place between the patient and the doctor, and that it was a drama, one could only see that this was in fact intersubjectivity in a situation that reminds us of that of the master and the slave. . . . As an anecdote, I can give you a very concrete example of this, that is, of its real efficacy. A year and a half ago there was [a conference] at Bonneval,[18] which is a small town, I think, in the department of Sarthe, remarkable in that it is dominated by an immense building that from a distance looks, for all the world, like a big château, because it sits on a flat plain; you see that from a distance: it's the psychiatric hospital, and in this psychiatric hospital Henri Ey reigns supreme.[19] He has occupied a place in the history of French psychiatry—I was going to say a place like that of Bergson in the history of French philosophy at the same period, but that would be to insult Ey because he played an extraordinarily positive role; he was, and I excuse myself for saying this, but it's very true—he was precisely the first great professor of French psychiatry, insofar as he taught French psychiatry that there was something outside the borders of France. Henri Ey can be considered a hero of the battle against provincialism, French provincialism in the theoretical domain that concerns psychiatry. In particular, he taught French psychiatry that a fellow named Jackson had existed somewhere,[20] no one knew where, but anyway, that he'd existed, that he'd written things, that they were important things, that people ought to know them, that they might have consequences, etc.

For years, in the comfort of his château at Bonneval, Ey has been periodically organizing a psychiatric conference in the course of which he sets forth his doctrine, which is a dynamico-psycho-organic doctrine, a kind of psychiatric Bergsonism that has, in fact, shed light on things and, besides, is inspired by Jackson; . . . and he provides an opportunity for people to express themselves. Obviously, he is no longer completely the intellectual guide of the younger generation. He was a contemporary of Lacan, since they studied together at Sainte-Anne; their meeting dates from that time; similarly, when they were there at Sainte-Anne they were roommates, and on the wall of their room this little phrase was written: "N'est pas fou qui veut" ("Not everyone is mad who wants to be")! For them, that was a whole program. In other words, madmen exist, but not everyone can be mad. . . . That was very important, because it meant: we have to take this seriously; it's not only negative, it's also positive—something positive is expressed in it. And Lacan has never denied this profound inspiration, all the less because he mentions Ey from time to time, to tell him: "Well, you remember, don't you, our common program, how are you getting on with "is not mad who wants to be?" From time to time he notes that Ey is behind on his program—it's not very difficult—and from time to time he also indulges in the malicious pleasure of allowing a public demonstration of this in front of Ey himself, in particular in the course of the last conference I'm talking about, which took place a year and a half ago, during which Laplanche gave his paper, written with Leclaire, on the unconscious and to which Ricoeur was invited.[21]

French psychiatry is defined in part by its need for philosophy, by an enormous consumption of philosophy. I'm not talking about medicine in general, but it is in any case certain that psychiatrists and psychoanalysts are among the biggest consumers on the French philosophical market. If philosophers did not exist in France, the publishers of philosophical works would survive them on the condition that psychiatry survived the philosophers. Ricoeur gave a talk that was, I think, very moving . . . anyway I heard so many people talking about it that I no longer dare say anything about it, because you've heard more about it than I have. But I want to say that what was at the heart of the encounter between Ricoeur and this world of psychiatry was in fact this encounter between the philosophical concepts of a philosophy of intersubjectivity and the analytical critique of therapy. What's going on? The psychoanalysts wonder: they have nothing for thinking about what goes on in therapy, in practice. And when someone from outside, who is a cultivated, intelligent, conscientious, honest, rigorous fellow like Ricoeur, comes to tell them: "Look, I think I can contribute something modest," in the hunger for theory that torments them they are moved, and all the more because Ricoeur is a man who lives these things, and because in the end perhaps the only collective misunderstanding that can characterize this historic encounter is that what was exchanged is not a concept traded for a practice— in other words, it was perhaps not theoretical concepts coming from philosophy that were exchanged against the analytic practice of therapy; I would say that one experience was traded for another. It's at that level that the thing could be real, that it made a convincing mark: they exchanged their experiences. The psychiatrists and psychoanalysts gave their experience, and Ricoeur gave his experience of the world of intersubjectivity, that is, a certain experience of moral practice, political practice, etc.: he was himself his own experience; his discourse was his own experience. What was exchanged was experience; I'm afraid that the concepts remained outside. I tell you this to show you what the situation is. It's not simply a ridiculous or polemical situation, it's a very real, very profound situation, and it forces us to inquire into what takes place on the psychoanalytic side, and what is happening, obviously, on the side of the other domains involved. That is, on the side of all the people who meet one another, including the most honest and authentic philosophers, since in this case Sartre, Merleau-Ponty, and Ricoeur are all absolutely above suspicion so far as authenticity is concerned.

So there you see in what domain the meeting that I talked about at the outset took place, and what principle I personally lived for a certain time, namely that psychology was psychoanalysis, that psychology didn't know it, but that, thank God, it was beginning to know it. The proof? It was spreading everywhere. And people thought that was just fine, that it sufficed to add a little theoretical consciousness to fix things and then it would be all right. From that moment on, a certain number of problems arise. The first one immediately strikes us: if in fact psychoanalysis is the essence of psychology—of psychology and of all the disciplines that depend on it; I'm taking psychology as an example, if you will—if psychoanalysis is the essence of psychology, what differentiates the domain of psychoanalysis from that of psychology? It's not easy to see what theoretical difference can be defined between psychoanalysis and psychology, between psychoanalysis and psychotherapeutic medicine, between psychoanalysis and psychiatry, etc. My teacher, Jean Guitton, used to tell us,[22] "if everything is pink, nothing is pink," and I have to say that this concept is certainly a fundamental concept that I owe him—one always has to recognize one's training; one has to be honest with regard to one's teachers; I incontestably owe him that concept—and it's the reflection on this concept that authorizes me to ask this question: if everything is psychoanalysis, nothing is psychoanalysis; if everything is psychology, nothing is psychology, so how can we ground the real differences? They're not imaginary, they really correspond to a difference in practice, because analytic practice is one thing, but psychotherapeutic practice is another: everyone will tell you that. Psychoanalysts who do psychotherapy will tell you that it's not the same thing at all, that quite different techniques are involved, etc.; the psychiatrist will tell you: "oh, so far as I'm concerned, the psychoanalysts . . . the concepts passed the border, but the techniques didn't at all, etc." There's a real difference.

The second theoretical problem, still in relation to "if everything is pink, nothing is pink," but this time applied to the agreement between psychoanalysis and philosophy. If the analytic situation is fundamentally identical to the situation of intersubjectivity, to the original situation of intersubjectivity, what difference is there between psychoanalysis and the philosophy of intersubjectivity? A real problem, not at all imaginary, because it is very precisely to this problem that Sartre's existential psychoanalysis responds. Sartre has undergone, or has claimed to have undergone, a psychoanalysis, has claimed to found a psychoanalysis, and he's not the only one. Binswanger,[23] in Germany, is not only a philosopher, but also a practitioner. They claimed to have created an existential psychoanalysis, that is, a psychoanalysis based theoretically on the identity of the doctor-patient relationship and the originary "for-others" (*Mitsein*), the originary intersubjectivity. That may very well be, but nonetheless it doesn't seem that that's quite how things are; Laplanche's article, for example, is definite about it: that's not what's happening in psychoanalytic reality itself.

To be clear and schematic at once, I have summed up the core of the problem in these two difficulties to tell you that Lacan is the only one who has answered these two fundamental questions. Lacan, obviously, is a figure who has existed for a long time, at least he exists for the world of psychoanalysis, and he also existed for the world of philosophy: you know that the first issue of *La Psychanalyse* contained a dialogue between Lacan and Hyppolite.[24] For a long time, Hyppolite attended Lacan's seminar, which is still going on, I point out—it's an eternal institution, one that reproduces itself—Wednesdays at 12:15 P.M., at the Sainte-Anne Psychiatric Hospital, women's ward. You should go once just to see, to realize on-site what goes on down there on Wednesdays at 12:15; it's not a convenient time, but it's the time for doctors, because they've finished their rounds.

Obviously Lacan existed a little in the world of philosophy. In his last lectures at the Collège de France, Merleau-Ponty cited him, but in the end he wasn't mentioned in any of Merleau-Ponty's fundamental works. Lacan is a historical phenomenon: we have to look into him. What is clear is that he's unintelligible for us Latins; he's enclosed behind a whole series of enigmas, hidden behind a whole series of coats of arms. In short, he presents himself in a form that is Gongoresque—since he has applied this adjective to himself—underneath a form theoretically and deliberately baroque, like a kind of wild beast: I believe that expression is not excessive; you have to have heard him scream to know that he is a man of an absolutely extraordinary aggressiveness, of a splendid maliciousness in which he certainly realizes himself as an individual who passed by way of surrealism. But the use of surrealism is not always exemplary; and that corresponds to something. To what? The hypothesis I present to you is that this aggressiveness is necessary because of the psychoanalytic milieu itself. I mean that the difficulties of psychoanalysis used to be between psychoanalysis, on the one hand, which was rejected by the cultural institutions, and the nonanalytic world, on the other. And when this takes place within the analytic world itself, that's another difficulty, because there it is not a question of a lack of understanding of psychoanalysis on the part of people who don't know Freud, but of a lack of understanding of psychoanalysis on the part of the very people who ought to know it. And in the current forms of the organization of the psychoanalytic world, that is, in the juridical, social, economic structures of the psychoanalytic world, I think there's no other way out than nastiness, on the one hand, and, on the other, a behavior of theoretical imposture through which, by pretending to say something incomprehensible, he says something perfectly clear, but to make it pass he needs to protect himself through the form of incomprehensibility he imposes on us. I think that for him this is a way of making his interlocutors feel stupid and that it gives them immediate proof that they don't understand anything they say; I think they need the immediacy of this proof in order to respect something that is hidden behind the very form of the inaccessibility of the discourse. If you go to Lacan's seminar, you'll see a whole series of people praying before a discourse that is unintelligible to them, unless they've frequented the master for a long time, or else— this is the very positive and absolutely inevitable aspect of his behavior—he uses the methods of intellectual terrorism, that is, he forces people to recognize that they don't understand what they're reading, that they don't understand because even the people who have a theoretical culture can't understand it, so all the more . . . In short, in these forms whose historical existence would have to be justified beyond Lacan's autobiographical reasons, something extremely important and extremely serious is going on, which I want to formulate very briefly: we can say that the theoretical work undertaken by Lacan is characterized by a radical, conscious, resolute refusal in which the resolution and the consciousness match the theoretical content. I mean that he's a guy who's resolute, not at all out of a decision made by the will, but on the basis of the theoretical certainty that what he says is founded. This resolution is manifested negatively and positively. It is manifested negatively by an implacable struggle against what we can only call the two trends that are currently dominant: the scientistic or mechanistic trend, so to speak, which connects psychoanalysis either to biology or psychophysiology or neurology or sociology, etc., that is, to objects into which it is absorbed, and, on the other hand, the trend of philosophical interpretation presently dominating the philosophical situation in France.

A radical rejection, but this radical rejection is not simply a rejection of revolt, as was the case with Politzer, that is, a rejection that simply sets something aside and then says: "we'll have to deal with that" but isn't up to thinking it through. Lacan doesn't offer us only the example of the concept and of the designation of the nonconcept, Lacan doesn't say we have to reject what exists from the theoretical point of view because reality is something else. He gives us two things: he gives us the nonconcept—excuse me, more exactly the concept and the non-concept at the same time; he's not content to say, "we mustn't think about that because it's false," but says instead, "here's how we can think about reality"; and he gives it to us through a return to Freud and a theoretical interpretation of Freud's texts. That's what we are going to work on.

Under such conditions, translating Lacan is a very important cultural necessity, and it interests us directly, if only in order to be able to read what he writes, of course.

If Lacan's attempt is well founded—I want to conclude with this point—it interests us to the greatest degree, from the theoretical point of view, for absolutely essential reasons. Because it's the whole domain we have envisaged with regard to the relations between psychoanalysis and psychology, that is, the whole domain of the human sciences in which the problem of what psychoanalysis is is raised—it's this whole domain that's at stake. I wouldn't say that everything depends on a reflection on psychoanalysis; I'd say, more precisely, that much depends on a reflection on psychoanalysis. Why? Because what exists for us, now, concretely, is not at all the problem of the relations between psychoanalysis and psychology or sociology, etc.: this problem is settled concretely by the actual relations that exist between psychoanalysis, psychology, etc. The world of the social sciences has no need at all for the work we are going to do this year—right here: it doesn't care about it at all, because theory doesn't interest it, it lives simply on things, consequences; it lives, and has long lived, in social psychology, anthropology, etc., not in the works that exist and in the people who write them. What interests *us* is the theoretical question that we are raising: what is the relation, not factual, concrete, actual, but theoretical, the relation de jure—I return now to what I said at the outset—between psychoanalysis and the human sciences? To answer that question we have to define the essence of psychoanalysis. In order to make our way into that world, we need the point that Archimedes asked for, in order to see further, that point of departure: we need an absolute point, a theoretical point; something, somewhere, has to be defined theoretically. The situation is such that this point is found in this world; in my opinion, there are two mooring points. The first . . . is the theoretical consequences of the problematic inaugurated by Marx, but that's something else. And the other is the work of someone who has nothing directly to do with Marx and who says, today we have a theoretical mooring point, and it's the only mooring point we have, not in the whole world, but very precisely in the world of psychology, in the world of the relation between psychology, psychiatry, etc., in the world that concerns the relation between psychology and psychoanalysis, and this mooring point is the possibility of a consistent, rigorous, valid, theoretical definition of psychoanalysis: that's what Lacan gives us.

2

Psychoanalysis and Psychology

WE'RE GOING to try to talk about the relation between psychoanalysis and psychology. That's a tall order because these relations are highly problematic: all we can hope to achieve is a definition of terms of which we can be relatively sure and on the basis of which we might be able to reach not the solution but at least an initial, relatively rigorous formulation of the problem. I would like to put this attempt, whose difficulty I have gauged in trying to give it these reference points, under the protection of this formula of Freud's: "Is it a mere accident that we have succeeded in providing a coherent and complete theory of the psyche only after having modified its definition?"[1] A formula that I would place alongside this other formula of Lacan's: "Saying that Freudian theory is a psychology is a crude equivocation."[2]

The problem I would like to try to address is the following: why does Freud's modification of the definition of psychoanalysis arrive at this conclusion, which radically separates psychoanalysis from psychology? To try to deal with this problem, to try to raise it, is practically to question the place of psychoanalysis. The presentations that you've heard so far have shown you that the question of the location of concepts within psychoanalysis was fundamental for their definition.[3] I think that the same can be said about psychoanalysis itself: the question of its location within the domain of the objectivity of existing sciences or possible sciences is essential for its own definition. And if I didn't want to avoid abusing an image here, I'd compare the description that Lacan gives of the subject of discourse, which is constantly haunted, as if by its absolute condition of possibility, by the empty site from which its discourse is uttered, with the situation of psychoanalysis itself, which, in Lacan's thought, is constantly haunted by the site that it could occupy in the domain of the objectivity constituted.

Where is psychoanalysis situated? What is its place? What is its location in a space that does not yet exist? What are its borders with existing disciplines? What are its nonborders with existing disciplines? These are the kinds of questions that constantly haunt Lacan's thought. And it's no exaggeration to say that they also haunted Freud's thought. What is equally striking, in both Lacan and Freud, is the following paradox. We find in Freud, as in Lacan, a twofold preoccupation: radically separating psychoanalysis from the discipline that claims to be the closest to it (psychology) and, on the contrary, trying to attach it to disciplines that are apparently distant from it (sociology, anthropology, or ethnology). This way formulating the problem and envisaging its solution might give new significance to certain texts of Freud's that have too often been considered simply aberrant, precisely insofar as people had a psychological conception of psychoanalysis: texts like *Totem and Taboo*, *The Future of an Illusion*, and *Civilization and Its Discontents*, that is, texts in which Freud tried to give a sociological status to concepts that seemed to be psychological. Perhaps at that point he brought them closer to their true place, but it may also be that, not having succeeded in locating the psychoanalytic concepts within psychoanalysis itself, he found it very difficult to locate psychoanalysis within an existing objectivity.

Why, in fact, is psychoanalysis seeking its place? I would like to propose the following hypothesis, which it seems impossible not to make after the presentations we've already heard concerning Lacan's interpretation of psychoanalysis[4]: if psychoanalysis actually represents the rise of a radically new scientific discipline, if it's true that Freud modified, as he says himself, the definition of the psyche, if it's true that Freud made a genuine scientific discovery, if then it's true that in psychoanalysis we're dealing with the rise of a new scientific discipline, that is, with the designation, specification, individuation of a new scientific object, to understand which new concepts are being proposed: if all that is true, in the case of Freud we're dealing with a phenomenon of which the history of culture was already aware. We're dealing with the rise of a scientific discipline that presents itself as totally new with regard to a field that was constituted earlier. We're dealing with the rise of a new truth, of a new knowledge, thus with the definition of a new object that breaks with the field constituted earlier: breaks with a field against the background of which this new discipline stands out. A field that is already occupied, that is an ideological field in which it has no place. . . . In the history of human culture we can observe phenomena of the same kind during the rise of a new scientific discipline, whether in the case of Greek mathematics, Galilean physics, Marx's theory of societies, etc. To the extent to which we're dealing with an epistemological break, with a rupture in the continuity with the earlier field, we're dealing with a phenomenon of rupture that contains in itself, like a real virtuality, a capacity to upset the field against which it stands out. That's the first point. But, at the same time, this rising up against the background of a field in which all the places are taken occurs under conditions such that the rise has a tendency to be contested and revoked by the field against the background of which it rises up. The rupture that a new scientific discipline introduces into a field in which all the places are taken, in fact, poses problems for the thinker or scientist who tries to define his new object, problems that are at first practically insoluble. This rupture has to be carried out within the field itself where it is supposed to intervene, practically in the language itself with which this new discipline has to break. That is why this remark of Freud's, "after having modified the definition of the psyche," is itself related to the psyche. And all the Freudian terminology itself relates to the concepts on the basis of which Freud conceives his discovery and with which he has to break. It's no accident that the psychology of the unconscious is defined as the negation of a psychology of consciousness. This legacy and this condition Freud cannot avoid weigh very heavily on the destiny of his thought.

The inevitable result of the rise of a new discipline against the background of an ideological field is that this ideological field tends to cancel the discipline, tends to deny the rupture, that is, to digest the new discipline that rises up as its own contradiction and its own challenge. And that's what's happening in the history of psychoanalysis, in which we see psychoanalysis disappearing under the impact of the mastication, psychoanalysis being digested either by biology or by psychology. The essential question will be why the discipline that digests psychoanalysis most of all is psychology. Why, in other words, did psychoanalysis rise up against the background of psychology? And why is it that this field is its most immediate field? The final consequence of this situation is that the recognition of this rupture, that is, of its specificity, is possible only through a total restructuring of the field against which this rupture rises up through a complete and real modification of this field, through the instauration of a new field, of a new border within this field: in short, through a redistribution of the places. That is why we can say that the problem of the place of psychoanalysis in the domain of the human sciences is a problem that arises in two ways. Psychoanalysis has no place in a field in which all the places are taken, and it is in that way that it will appear to be outside the field, as not having a border with it, as occupying an empty place. The second aspect of the problem of the place of psychoanalysis is that psychoanalysis cannot occupy a place in this field unless this field is itself completely restructured, that is, unless its topology is completely changed by it, unless the very nature of this field is modified by it. Does psychoanalysis alone suffice to modify the topology of this field, that is, to change its nature and its internal divisions? That's an open question. Lacan thinks, in fact, that psychoanalysis can restructure the field on which it has risen up. That may be beyond its possibilities.

We're going to try to see how, against the background of the existing field, we can make an initial attempt to locate psychoanalysis. Here I've made a somewhat schematic drawing that represents what might be called an initial attempt to locate psychoanalysis.[5] What we've learned from Lacan's interpretation is that psychoanalysis concerns the little child's becoming human, that is, his integration into culture through the defiles of the signifier, that is, through the defiles of culture itself and the a priori culture that conditions any acculturation of this little biological being that is a little human biological being [*sic*]. This little biological being becomes a child starting from the moment he has crossed the boundary of the Oedipus complex, from the moment he is integrated into the machinery, that is, into the distribution of roles that are imposed on him by the kinship structures that are reflected in the order of the signifier through which he expresses his need in the form of a demand. The problem is then the following: what does the little human being encounter when he achieves the state of little human child? If psychoanalysis concerns, in fact, this passage from the biological to the cultural, the passage from the little biological being to the little human child, what does the little human being encounter when he enters culture after having passed through the defile of the signifier? In the current state of the field of the human sciences, it might be thought that he encounters a psychological reality, that he will become a psychological subject, and that psychology will be the point where the individual human is integrated into culture, that is, into human relations. Psychology, which will then be replaced by a new discipline: psychosociology. . . . I can give you an example of this interpretation—about which, I hasten to say, you all know this already: that it's abstract; the example of the interpretation proposed in the ideology of the eighteenth and nineteenth centuries, particularly in the ideology based on Condillac, that of wild children. If you have an opportunity to read Dr. Itard's reports on the wild boy of Aveyron . . . you can find them in Lucien Malson's *Les Enfants sauvages* where they have just been published.[6]

You know that the eighteenth century took an interest in this problem of the passage from nature to culture; and one of the examples on which eighteenth-century reflection focused was that of so-called wild children: wolf-children, calf-children, pig-children, etc.—that is, children who were picked up in the woods, who lived with animals, and who were found in a state in which there was nothing human about them, but instead they had an animal behavior that made them seem to be little wolves, little bears, etc. Here's what we can say about the essential characteristics of these wild children, although it's obviously pretty difficult to really verify it, because it's possible that a certain number of perceptions—ideological perceptions—played a role in defining these characteristics. The first characteristic is that they go on all fours; the second is that they do not speak and almost never learn to speak, a very interesting phenomenon; the third is that they show no sexual desire; the fourth is that they cannot recognize themselves in a mirror; the fifth is that they can't smile. These characteristics, which were summed up not by eighteenth-century philosophers but by anthropologists who have reflected on these examples, are perhaps not without interest insofar as a whole series of contemporary studies, in particular those of Spitz,[7] have connected all these phenomena that an experimental child psychology can observe and that play an essential role in Lacan's and Freud's thinking about the phenomena we are studying.

Let's take the example of the wild boy of Aveyron studied by Dr. Itard, who worked and taught at an institute for the deaf and dumb (quite near here, as it happens) and had been assigned to study the wild boy of Aveyron by the minister of interior, at the time,[8] who was eager to promote the sciences. What is extremely interesting about this case is that Dr. Itard implemented a pedagogy based precisely on the hypothesis that this wild child was a biological being who had to be integrated into society by teaching him human behaviors as if he were a psychological subject. In other words, the pedagogy Itard applied was a Condillacian pedagogy that tried to restore the continuity between the biological individual and the psychological subject. The most interesting example, because it challenges the concept that is essential to our reflection here, is that of language, is that of the attempts Itard made to teach the child to speak. He got very disappointing results, but what's interesting is to see how he reflects on his own disappointment. The first thing Itard noted was that this young savage was sensitive to sounds that were completely insignificant for a cultivated man, for example the sound that is made when shelling a nut, but he was completely insensitive to a rifle shot fired behind his back, and completely insensitive to the human voice. And the only human sound, the only human vowel that he finally recognized, was the vowel *o*—that's why Itard gave him the name of Victor:

One day when he was in the kitchen cooking potatoes, two people were having a lively argument behind him, without his seeming to pay them the slightest attention. A third person came in and joined the discussion, beginning all his remarks with these words: "Oh, that's different." I noticed that every time that person uttered his favorite exclamation "Oh," the wild boy of Aveyron's head whipped around. That evening, at bedtime, I carried out a few experiments in this intonation, and I got more or less the same results. I reviewed all the other simple intonations known under the term of "vowels," but without success. This preference for the "O" led me to give him a name that ended with this vowel. I chose that of *Victor*. He has kept his name, and when it is uttered in a loud voice, he seldom fails to turn his head or come running up.

And here's the most interesting thing: "It may also be for the same reason that later on he understood the meaning of the negation *non* ("no"), which I often use to correct him when he makes mistakes in his little exercises."[9]

There we have, so to speak, the identification of a conditioned reflex. And our good doctor, after he'd succeeded in establishing this point of contact, this mooring, with a vowel, tried to develop language: "I had reason to think that the vowel 'O,' having been the first heard, would be the first pronounced, and I found it extremely fortunate for my plan that this simple utterance was, at least so far as the sound was concerned, the sign of one of this child's most ordinary needs."

There we have the theoretical basis on which this pedagogy was to be developed: the word is conceived here as the sign of a need. A whole philosophy of language is implicit here: a sign of a need, the need of an individual, of a psychological subject who is going to be defined by his needs, and who will have to use language as a system of signs serving as a mediation of his needs. And here's what's going to happen:

> However, I was unable to derive any advantage from this favorable coincidence. When he was very thirsty, I held before him a vessel full of water, crying frequently, "eau," "eau"; then I gave the vessel to another person who uttered the same word in front of him, and getting it back from him by the same means; all in vain. The poor fellow twisted all about, waved his arms around the vessel in an almost convulsive manner, produced a kind of whistling sound, but articulated not a single sound. It would have been inhumane to persist any longer. I changed the subject, but not the method. I tried working with the word "lait" (milk).
>
> (164–65)

The word *lait* is the first word that this child pronounced, and that completely disconcerted our good doctor-philosopher:

> On the fourth day of this second attempt, I succeeded in getting what I wanted, and I heard Victor pronounce distinctly, though admittedly in a somewhat crude way, the word "lait," which he repeated almost immediately. It was the first time that an articulate sound emerged from his mouth, and I heard it with the deepest satisfaction. However, one thought greatly diminished the advantage of this first success. It was only at the moment when, giving up hope of succeeding, I had just poured

the milk into the cup he held out to me, that the word "lait" escaped him with the greatest demonstrations of pleasure; and it was again only after I had poured him some more as a kind of reward that he uttered it a second time. One sees why this kind of result was far from fulfilling my intentions; the word uttered, instead of being the sign of a need, was, in relation to the time when it was articulated, only an empty exclamation of joy. If this word had come out of his mouth before he was given what he wanted, then it was done; Victor would have grasped the true use of the word.

(That is: Victor would have grasped the philosophy of the Enlightenment's conception, Condillac's conception, of the psychological subject, and would have become a little Condillacian.) "One point of communication was being established between him and me, and more rapid progress flowed from this first success" (164–65). You see the whole philosophy of language that is implicit in this practice: the subject defined by his needs, the mediation of language as sign, the sign in unequivocal relation with the thing, and communication established between two subjects by means of language, a system of signs in direct relation with the subject. "Instead of all that, I had just obtained only an expression, meaningless for him and useless for us, of the pleasure he felt. At most, it was a vocal sign, the sign of the possession of the thing. But that, I repeat, did not establish any relationship between us; it was soon to be disregarded precisely because it was useless for the individual's needs and subject to numerous anomalies, like the ephemeral and variable feeling of which it had become the indication" (165–66). Nonetheless, later on Itard noticed that the word *lait* was pronounced by Victor as *la, li, lli* (a little like *gli* in Italian, that is, with a rolled *l*), and he wondered if that was not related to a certain little girl ("named Julie, a young lady of eleven or twelve who came to spend Sundays at the home of Mme Guérin, her mother. It is certain that on that day the exclamations 'li' and 'lli' became more frequent, and were even heard, her governess reported, during the night at a time when there was reason to think that everyone was sound asleep. We cannot determine with precision the cause and value of this last fact"; 166–67).

I have quoted this text at length to give you an example of an interpretation in which this becoming-human of the biological subject is interpreted in relation to a whole ideology of the psychological subject defined by his needs, and language comes in simply as a theory of the sign in relation to the thing, needs being themselves related to the thing: the thing has to be obtained by language as a means of communication with another who will give it to the child. Need is determined, it is expressed, in a sign that passes through another person who gives the thing, and the thing is directly related to the need. The circle is thus completed, but it causes the presence of two subjects to appear: the one who speaks (the subject who utters) and the one who understands language and causes to appear a particular status of language in which there is an unequivocal relation between the sign and the thing signified, between the signifier and the thing signified. There you have the whole ideological background, which involves an imaginary machinery: that of two subjects communicating through language, this means of communication between two subjects being itself a means of signifying a thing that is signified by the linguistic signifier. That is, you find in all this a structure in which the subjects communicate through language, itself in direct relation with the thing, the thing being itself in direct relation with the needs of language. Everything is flattened out: the subject and his needs are one and the same, and it's through this twofold identity that communication is possible.

That is the background of the ideological conception with which the break in modern linguistics was to take place, a break that Lacan was to take advantage of. This flattening, this horizontal character of the two subjects in their alterity, of two subjects defined by their needs, in other words, the identity of the subject and his needs, on the one hand, and, on the other, the identity of the sign, of the signifier and the signified—all that forms a similar structure and belongs to the same fundamental problematic. That is the basis on which the subject is defined as a psychological subject: and it is this imaginary machinery, this imaginary theory that Itard tries to use to introduce the little biological being to the quality of a psychological subject. And it doesn't work. It doesn't work, but, on the other hand, he observes phenomena as aberrant as the one through which an expression turns out to be related to manifestations of joy, with a whole sort of show that can also be related to the presence of a certain little girl associated with these words, etc. All these phenomena are aberrant for him and don't enter into his conception.

All that to give you an idea of the cultural background, the ideological backdrop, against which we can try to conceive this becoming-human of the little human animal. Thanks to what Lacan has explained to us, we know that, so far as we're concerned, that's not how it works. We know that in analytic practice the psychoanalyst is dealing, in the subject facing him in therapy, with what we can call the traces of this archeology, that is, with the currently present traces of this archeology, that is, with the currently present traces of what happened at the crucial moment of the integration of the little human being into the cultural world. And what's crucial—this is what Lacan insists on, and it's his great discovery—is that this becoming-human that is going to be represented for you by this vector,[10] "passage from the biological to the cultural," is in reality the effect of the action of the cultural on the biological. What is represented here by this vector must actually be represented by another vector: it is the cultural that acts on the biological, as the condition of the possibility of integrating the little human animal. Instead of dealing with this "biology → culture" vector, we're dealing with a very different structure in which culture produces this forward movement: we're dealing with an inversion of the determination.

It's through the action of culture on the little biological human being that his integration into culture takes place. Thus it's not the becoming-human of the little human being that we're dealing with, it's the action of culture, constantly, on a little being other than culture itself, which culture transforms into a human being. That is, we're actually dealing with a phenomenon of investment whose vector is apparently oriented toward culture, whereas in fact it is culture that constantly precedes itself, absorbing the being that is to become a human subject.

The second consequence of Lacan's reflection is that what precedes the becoming-human of the little human being isn't psychology, it's not the psychological subject, but what he calls "the order of the symbolic," or what I would call, if you will, the law of culture. It's the law of culture that determines the passage to culture itself. I believe that we have to understand it in its full dimension. And first of all by opposing it to what this fundamental discovery opposed itself: a problematic of the relation between nature and culture that is reflected in an ideology of which I gave you an example regarding Itard and that is reflected in the form of the psychological development of the little biological being. This is the famous problem of eighteenth-century philosophy, that of the transition from the state of nature to the state of society. This problem is raised in a paradoxical way that Rousseau pertinently criticized. All the terms are present, for example, in Rousseau's critique of Hobbes. In the philosophy of the transition from nature to society, the ideology of the eighteenth century represents this transition as one between two states: from one distinct state to another distinct state. And if you've kept this critique in mind, the sense of Rousseau's criticism of Hobbes is to bring out the ideological circle involved in this conception.

What is the sense of Rousseau's criticism of Hobbes? Rousseau says to Hobbes, and more generally to all the natural-law philosophers, that they've pretended to imagine a being that is only nature, whereas in reality they've projected onto the state of nature the structures of the state of society. They've pretended to represent as noncultural a being that in fact they've endowed with all the cultural properties necessary to conceive the state of society from which they've abstracted him. That's the sense of Rousseau's introduction to his *Discourse on the Origin of Inequality Among Men*. And Rousseau's criticism is extremely profound insofar as he brings out a truth that we can still endorse today, namely that what the philosophers of nature conceived in the passage from nature to society is simply the conditions of the possibility of the existence of society, conceived in the form of nonsociety. The subject who is conceived as "man in the state of nature" is represented as endowed with all the attributes, potential or developed, that actually belong to a subject of the world of society, that is, to a cultural subject. And that is doubtless why an important revolution in the thought of Rousseau in the second *Discourse* consists precisely in not conceiving the problem of the transition from nature to society in terms of the individual, but in terms of the species: not asking, as Condillac had, what a given individual becomes, how a given individual might develop, but instead conceiving the development of society as a social phenomenon. That is, he conceives the permanent antecedence of culture or of society with respect to its own cultural development, conceives the fact that society always precedes itself. Now it is such fundamental truth (which Rousseau later abandons precisely in the attempt to represent, in the form of a natural man, the political and social ideal to which he is attached) that we find in Lacan's reflection. Culture always precedes itself, and it is this precedence, this perpetual antecedence of culture with respect to itself, that is represented by this circle. And, to tell the truth, we have to note that if we take things a little seriously, in psychoanalysis we are never dealing with the direct observation of this antecedence of culture with [respect to] itself at the moment when the infant becomes a human child, when the little biological being becomes a human child. In reality, we are always dealing with an ulterior phenomenon, with a phenomenon that is situated within culture, because in the case of analytic therapy it is a question of a practice addressed to a human being who has been a human child: when we talk about the becoming-human of the little human biological being we are dealing with a first recurrence. It is this first recurrence that raises so many problems for classical psychoanalytic theory, which is psychological in inspiration, in particular the problem of whether the recollection at work in therapy is a phenomenon of reality, whether it corresponds to realities. This phenomenon of recurrence, which corresponds, for example, to the famous problem of whether the primal scene, which Freud said might be so traumatizing, should be considered a historically real scene or a fantasy. A difficulty that we also find in the problem of abreaction and in the problem of regression. In other words, the problem of recollection in associations, in rules, in interpretations, the problem of abreaction, and the problem of regression, three essential concepts on which Lacan reflects, are problems connected with the fundamental fact that the recollection at work in analytic practice is not taken seriously in psychological theory. In other words, it is because what takes place in analytic practice is not seen as taking place, in fact, within a constituted cultural world, in a subject who is already a subject of determined society, a subject of culture, that all these problems are posed in terms of the relations between the biological and the psychological. All these false problems that Lacan points out (the problems of recollection, abreaction, regression, etc.) are problems that arise from neglecting the fact that what is conceived as the antecedent of culture with respect to itself in the human development of the little biological being is in fact situated within culture itself. In other words, the precession of culture in its relation to biology is a precession of culture with respect to itself that is situated at the cultural level in psychoanalytic practice.

It is here that another consequence appears. How is it possible to conceive the identity of the signification of this precession of culture with respect to itself that is at work in analytic therapy in relation to the retrospective localization that is assigned in recollection, abreaction, regression, etc., as concerning the becoming-human of the little biological being? The problem raised here is absolutely insoluble in a psychological theory of the unconscious, and it's a problem that Lacan confronts and resolves, it seems to me, by making it clear that it is precisely through the insistence of relationships constituted in the whole cultural development of the cultural being from the time when he is a little child through the conditions of possibility of this insistence in language, that is, in the order of the symbolic (whose meaning we will have to explain later on), that the possibility of this recurrence is founded. In other words, this recurrence is possible because temporality, which it is impossible to conceive with a psychological subject, is subjected to conditions of possibility that are not the social frameworks of memory, in the sense in which Halbwachs understood them,[11] but are identical with the structure of the symbolic that is subject to the model of language. This is because the cultural development of the little human being who has become an adult, subject to therapy, is subject to this condition of possibility as a condition of the possibility of his own temporality, because it is possible to found this recurrence, and to speak of the human development of the little biological being at the time of the therapy, that is, at a time when this little biological being is a human being and is no longer anything but a human being.

It's on that basis that we can grasp the relations between psychoanalysis and psychology: on the basis of this paradoxical situation and on the basis of its misunderstandings. I would like to give you a few clues—you already know the gist—that manifest in a concrete way the paradoxical situation of psychoanalysis in the field in which it arises. I was saying that the emergence of a new scientific discipline, which is destined by its very novelty to express itself in an existing terminology, that is, to stand out against this background, produces an ambiguous situation, particularly the temptation to relapse into this background; in any case, it produces, on the part of the ideological field against which it stands out, the temptation to absorb it. That is the second point of this presentation, in which I would like to talk about psychology, giving you two examples of psychology's attempts to digest psychoanalysis and trying to reflect very schematically on what this psychology that tries to absorb psychoanalysis is.

The first example of psychology's attempt to digest psychoanalysis is the one made by Anna Freud. In an issue of the *Revue française de psychanalyse* devoted to honoring Freud, there is an article by Anna Freud entitled "La contribution de la psychanalyse à la psychologie génétique."[12] If you're patient enough to look at it—it's not very long, it's very schematic, it's very caricatured, it's very representative . . . it can be summed up this way: Anna Freud's whole effort consists in conceiving psychoanalysis as the interiority of the biological or psychological in order to relate it to the social.[13] All the preexisting categories are retained, are naively retained; it's just that the psychological subject becomes a subject that has a biological interiority—that of the "id," of the instincts, of drives, of tendencies, etc.—that is going to be related to society. Whence arises a whole series of conflicts. Psychology becomes the "ego," which is the central category of Anna Freud's whole theory. She declares, for example, that "in the history of psychoanalysis, genetic investigation has evolved from the study of libidinal development to that of inhibiting forces, it has established the description of the two main, simultaneous and parallel lines that the human personality follows in its growth."[14] The human personality appears to be double, and it is the interest of psychoanalysis to have doubled the former psychological subject with a new internal reality: "The genetic data drawn from this twofold observation in the course of analysis permit us to enlarge our knowledge of the origin and development of the two aspects of an individual's personality. Regarding instinctual tendencies, this work has in its time allowed us to reconstruct the pregenital phases of libidinal development . . . and later on [the phases] of the concomitant development of aggressive tendencies. Regarding the ego and the superego, it has allowed us gradually to understand their origin and to show these aspects of the personality." And here's the key sentence: "It is on the basis of a simple, central point, the consciousness of sensations of pleasure and displeasure, that the complex organization of the ego responsible for important functions (such as perceptions, memory, reality-testing, the synthesis of experience, the mastery of motor functions) and the major task of serving as an intermediary between the external world and the internal world develops; and so far as the superego is concerned, it represents and imposes the moral requirements of the social environment within the individual personality."[15] In this personality, in this psychological subject of Anna Freud's,[16] we are dealing with what she calls a double personality, with two fundamental elements of the personality: the id, which is biological (the drives, the instincts, etc.), and the ego, which is in a conflictual relationship with the id, that is, it tries to defend itself against its aggression, against its excesses of aggressivity, etc., and which exists, at the same time, in relation to reality. The ego then occupies an extremely difficult position, because it is obliged to synthesize the id's aggressions with reality's requirements. Reality is twofold: it is both the perceived reality, in other words, the objective world, that is, the norms, that is, ethics. These norms and ethics are to be represented in the form of the superego, which always challenges, in the same way, the relation between a subject and an external reality—this external reality being that of the objective world, of the world that can be perceived, and at the same time the reality of ethical norms, etc. The conflict between the subject and external reality develops within this subject, which includes three agencies. That is to say, psychoanalysis has simply introduced two new dimensions into the interior of the subject, dimensions that are only the reflection, the establishment, the repercussion, so to speak, on the basis of the subject still conceived as the "ego," the central subject of its relationships with reality. A reality that is twofold: both theoretical reason and practical reason, and is thus found invested within the subject in the form of the ego: the ego being this central position that tries to remain central, that tries to maintain its position against the aggressions of the id or of social reality (in the form of the super-ego or the objective external world). It is on that basis that Anna Freud's theory of "the ego's defense mechanisms" is developed.[17] And on that basis a whole tendency of psychoanalysis is centered on the "ego's defense mechanisms," that is, on the mechanisms through which the subject succeeds in keeping itself centered on the ego, which is the function of a synthesis at once theoretical and practical.

This interpretation of psychoanalysis, this psychologizing theory of psychoanalysis, leads to important technical consequences that Lacan constantly points out, particularly to the primacy of the analysis of resistances. That is to say, to the primacy of the resistances that the ego uses as defense mechanisms to protect itself, to protect its synthetic function, against all the external world's aggressions, and especially against the capacities for aggression represented for it by the psychoanalyst, who is an ego stronger than its own that threatens the internal equilibrium of its own unity. I won't linger on this theory, which leads to absolutely extraordinary consequences, because the problem finally ends up, in Anna Freud's work,[18] in a kind of total obscurity regarding the possibilities of an encounter between the ego's mechanisms and those of the id. It's simply by chance that we happen to observe a certain number of constant relationships between the id and the ego, etc. It amounts to a veritable dissolution of all of Freudian theory.

As a second example of the digestion of psychoanalysis by psychology, we can cite the example of Lagache. Lagache tries to give an explanation of Lacan's "Rome Discourse."[19] And he gives an explanation of Lacan's relationship in terms of existential philosophy, appealing specifically to Sartre and dissolving the reality of psychoanalytic theory in a fashionable psychological philosophy that, in truth, reconstitutes in a modern form the old psychological temptation to which Anna Freud yielded.[20] We can say that Anna Freud represents, so to speak, the old classical psychology, that of the ego as a moral subject based on a duality between the interiority of the subject and the exteriority of the objective world, that the latter is the perceived objective world of social norms, the ethical norms dominant in society, society's moral demands. And we can say, on the contrary, that Lagache's attempt gives the psychological subject a new status in which this exteriority is reabsorbed into a philosophy of existence, into a philosophy of consciousness, into a philosophy of intentionality. It is extremely amusing to see that Lagache's whole effort to interpret Lacan tends to explain to Lacan that Lacan's main contribution consists in deobjectifying psychology, that is, in disalienating the subject, of dereifying it, etc., whereas, in reality,

Lacan's effort consists in an elaboration of objectivity that is the precondition of any understanding of the subject. What is also interesting is that Lagache, in his response to Lacan, shows his own theory of the doctor-patient relationship by resorting to a term that Lacan had quoted from some psychoanalyst or other: psychoanalysis is a "two-body psychology";[21] it's a psychology that questions two subjects, one opposite the other. And it resolves [the problem] in a psychology of intersubjectivity, in a psychology that causes another kind of subject to appear: not the psychological subject with its biological background, as in Anna Freud, but the subject as a subject of meaning, the subject in which the structures revealed by Lacan are dissolved into simple structures of meaning (meaning for a consciousness), that is, into a veritable psychology of intentionality. And it's no accident that Lagache connects up with Politzer, who had tried, precisely, to substitute for the structures of the Freudian unconscious a psychology of first-person drama, that is, a psychology of consciousness.

What is the essential criticism Lacan addresses to psychology's attempts to digest psychoanalysis? His essential criticism bears on the following point: every attempt made by psychology to digest psychoanalysis is based on a confusion between the subject and the ego, that is, on a misunderstanding of the function of the ego in the subject, which is precisely to be a function of recognition and misunderstanding. Lacan's second fundamental objection is that the psychology at work in this attempt to refute psychoanalysis is also based on a confusion between structure and meaning, a confusion that is possible only on the basis of a philosophy of consciousness. In other words, the psychoanalysis presented in this psychological form undergoes the fundamental structure of psychology, that is, the fundamental structure according to which the human subject is supposed to be identical with the human ego, that is, it is supposed to have the centered structure of the human ego. On that basis, the essential theme of Lacan's criticism can be put in the following way: if we reduce psychoanalysis to the typical structure of psychology, we no longer understand what the unconscious is. As soon as we try to reduce psychoanalysis to psychology, the unconscious becomes an interior of consciousness; either a biological id, something that falls short of the ungraspable subject interior to the subject, or simply the experienced but occulted sense, the nonsense that is always the risk taken by meaning experienced in the intentionality of consciousness. That is the fatal nature of this centering of the subject on the ego, that is, of the subjection of the structure of the subject to the imaginary structure of the ego, and in that way, in the very measure that the unconscious becomes immanent to the psychological subject, this essential dimension of the unconscious that is its transcendence is lost: a transcendence manifest in the Freud's own works, insofar as the unconscious is sought as something beyond the subject, conceived as something beyond the psychological subject. This transcendence of the subject is what modern psychology, and in particular Sartrean or Politzerian psychology, seek in intersubjectivity. The transcendence of the unconscious is conceived—for example by Lagache, after Politzer—as that of the immanence of the alter ego: the unconscious is invested in what is conceived as the condition of possibility of its transcendence, that of a transcendental intersubjectivity, at the very level of the experienced. It is there, obviously, that the most important point is situated: this transcendental intersubjectivity, which appears as the site of the unconscious in a psychology of the Politzerian or Sartrean type, or inspired by phenomenology, this intersubjectivity, conceived as the transcendental condition of possibility of psychological alterity, has the same structure as that of the psychological subject. This is the point that we have to try to show with a little precision. In both cases—whether it is a matter of an interiorization of the unconscious, in the form of the biological or in the form of meaning, or of a recognition and its transcendence in the form of a transcendental intersubjectivity—we seem to be dealing with the same structure through which the real structure of the subject is subjected to the imaginary structure of the ego, that is, to the same centered structure.

Why does psychology present itself in this form? That's the point I want to examine now by asking: what is psychology? Where does psychology come from? What is its past? What are its arrears? What are the scars that it still bears today? Here it's not a question of producing a historical study: I simply want to try to give two or three clues preparatory to a possible study.

The very idea of a psychology presupposes a certain number of fundamental structures that make it possible. These fundamental structures are those that identify three realities of differing status: the individual, the subject, and the ego. Psychology is possible only through the identification of these three terms, that is, through the theoretical presupposition that the subject is an individual possessing the structure of an ego. This constitution supposes and imposes this identity as real. But it suffices to inquire into the status of the three terms thus presented to see that they're not at the same level, in other words, that they don't have the same content, and that this identity lumps together three signifiers that don't have the same signification, that can't be identified. The individual is a concept that can have a meaning in the domain of biology, that can have a meaning in the division of labor, in the division of social functions. The subject is a concept that also has a meaning in the social division of labor and particularly as a subject to which a certain number of behaviors are imputed, whether they are moral behaviors or political behaviors. It is no accident that the subject designates the one that is subjected, whereas in the classical function of psychology the subject designates the one who is active. It is this reversal, for example, that creates the whole paradox of a psychology whose origin is manifestly political: the subject is the one who is subjected to an order, who is subjected to a master, and who is at the same time conceived in psychology as being the origin of its own actions. This means that it is a subject of imputation, that is, that it is the one that has to justify its own acts, its own behavior, to a third party. And if we consider the ego, which is the third term in this identification, we see that, itself, it appears connected with quite different structures, with a quite different problematic. It is especially connected with a properly philosophical problematic that develops beginning in the seventeenth century, with a problematic that makes the subject appear as an ego, that is, as a subject of truth, as a subject of objectivity.

We can conclude from this, in a first approximation, that the three terms whose radical identification is the presupposition of any psychology are in truth three heterogeneous terms. The biological individual, whose place can be assigned as such either in the biological field or in the field of the division of labor, that is, in the field of the division of roles in society, is one thing. The subject is a subject of imputation, that is, he is the one who has to obey orders and must justify his obedience and his acts, whether these orders are moral, political, religious, etc. And the ego corresponds to a third function, which is a "veritative" function, a function of synthesis, a function of objectivity. So it is the synthesis, if you wish, of these three conditions, of these three objects, that is the condition of possibility of any psychology. If we try to see what there is behind this condition of possibility, proposed to psychology as if it could be taken for granted, if we try to see on what condition a psychology could be constituted, we'll find ourselves confronted by rather curious and rather interesting phenomena. I'd like to show that a psychology is made possible as the by-product of a political ideology, a moral ideology, or a philosophical ideology, and that this by-product can have a twofold character: either that of a normative pathology of the ideology that produced it or that of a mirror foundation (*fondement en miroir*) of the ideology that produced it.

As an example of the first case, I shall take Plato. Obviously, the concept of psychology is a recent concept, since it appeared only in the eighteenth century, and the French word did not appear until Charles Bonnet used in around 1750.[22] We know that this term is owed to Wolff,[23] but it was introduced in France by Charles Bonnet. Thus it is paradoxical to speak of psychology with regard to Plato, since in fact psychology was never thematized as a discipline during the classical period of the Greek philosopher. All the same, I would like to point out that, as early as the age of Greek philosophy, structures were established that were later to be adopted and that appear as conditions of the possibility of a psychology. So far as Plato is concerned, I would like to take the well-known example of *The Republic*, that of the tripartite division of classes referring to the tripartite division within the subject. Plato, inquiring into man, tells us we can read in capital letters what the nature of man is by reading it in society; it's easier to read a text in capital letters than in small letters. To understand man, he refers us to the structure of society, and when he studies the structure of society he refers us to man, that is, he refers us to a human subject in which the structure of society is to be founded. Now, this subject is itself conceived as constituted by a tripartite structure, the *epithumía*, the *thumós*, and the *noûs*. If we analyze Plato's procedure, we see that this human subject, conceived as constituted by a tripartite structure, is in fact the by-product of the political problems that Plato is trying to resolve. It is simultaneously the reflection of these political problems in the individual and the expression of this political problem presented as its solution and its foundation. It is a foundational pathology: it's because, in fact, there are three agencies in man, the *epithumía*, the *thumós*, and the *noûs*, that a true order can be established in society, or, on the contrary, a confused disorder can reign instead. It is the confusion of these three agencies in the individual that can lead to the confusion of classes in society. We see here that the tripartite structure in the human subject is expected to resolve the problem of the division of classes in society. But this transfer of the difficulty, presented in the form of a solution, leads to paralogisms that it is amusing to follow in the detail of *The Republic*: particularly in the fact that everyone being presented as constituted by a tripartite structure; we see that, in accord with the classes, each person is actually reduced to one of the functions of this tripartite structure. The artisan is only *epithumía*; if, by chance, the artisan were something other than *epithumía*, disorder would ensue; the guardian is only *thumós*, and if, by chance, he was *noûs* or *epithumía*, disorder would ensue; and the king, the philosopher-king, is only *noûs*. There is a contradiction between the structure of the human being and the function this structure is supposed to perform in society; Plato's solution is to simply substitute for the tripartite structure a hierarchy among the functions in the human subject, that is, to immediately invest a possible psychology with a moral. It is the ordering of the three agencies in the human subject that appears as the condition of possibility of the ordering of the classes in society. We see here what role is played by the establishment of this structure of a possible psychology in Plato's work: to justify the pathology of politics, to justify the fact that the social order is not what it should be, and, at the same time, to found a social order that would be what it should be. But this social order cannot be founded as such in an individual except on the condition of denying the objective meaning of the structures established that could found a psychology and of transforming it immediately into morals. Politics becomes morals in the individual; morals being, in the guise of the constitution of a subject that can be the object of an objective study, nothing but the establishment of an order that, in the subject, realizes the condition of possibility and the foundation of the order that are supposed to be worked out in society.

It is in another very different domain that the role of the establishment of the structure of the ego in Cartesian philosophy is played out. What can the possibility of a psychology be in Cartesian philosophy? It can't be a psychology of the ego, of the *ego cogito*, insofar as the subject of the ego is here a subject of objectivity, that is, a subject of truth. On the other hand, we see that psychology is made possible in Descartes as the pathology, itself liable to represent the flip side of a normalcy, which allows the fully justified exercise of the ego of objectivity. In other words, psychology is made possible in Descartes in order to account for error, to account for inattention, to account for confusion, to account for the confusion in inattention, to account for the taking of liberty in the appearances of the sensible and the body, that is, to account for the confusion of the subject of objectivity with its contrary in order account for the confusion of the truth in error, of the misunderstanding of the truth in error. The psychological subject that appears here as the precondition of the subject of objectivity is the subject of error; at the same time, it is the subject of error being able to convert itself into a subject of objectivity. Psychology can thus be founded in Descartes as concerning the concept of the nonconcept of the ego, as concerning the possibility that the ego is not this transparency itself that constitutes it as a subject of truth, as a subject of objectivity: that is, as concerning its own past. That is why it is on the basis of the veritative functions of the ego as subject of objectivity that the fundamental functions of the psychological subject are determined negatively: memory, attention, haste, prejudice, imagination, feeling—all categories through which Descartes conceives the possible pathology that is the flip side of the normalcy of the subject of objectivity. Descartes's *Traité des passions de l'âme* is a treatise on theoretical pathology, on gnoseopathology, and it is, at the same time, a treatise on ideal normality: the psychological subject becomes the site where the relation between the subject of truth and the subject of error is played out. And it is in a concept like that of attention, in a concept like that of freedom (which appears as the content of this concept of attention) that the destiny of the psychological subject is played out, a destiny that is to be precisely the shadow of the subject of objectivity, that is, to be its flip side and, at the same time, its possibility. The pathology appears here as the pathology of the psychological subject; the psychological subject appears here as the pathological subject, as the possibility of the pathology of the subject of objectivity, a pathology that can be immediately converted into normalcy by the essential function that is given to this subject: the function of convertibility that is freedom. From this point of view, it would be extremely interesting to see what happens, for example, to the *Traité des passions* in Spinoza, on the basis of the criticism that Spinoza makes precisely of the Cartesian *cogito*, of this ego that appears as the center of the *cogito*. The question would be whether Spinoza's abandonment of the subject of objectivity as the condition of possibility of any affirmation of truth doesn't lead to a radical modification of the subject of this pathology of truth. In other words, the question would be whether the status of the subject of the passions of the soul in Descartes, which is defined as this possibility of an alternative between error and truth, which is thus conceived on the basis of the subject of objectivity, is not profoundly modified in Spinoza precisely on the basis of the suppression of this subject of objectivity and whether the *Traité des passions de l'âme*, instead of opening the way toward a psychology, that is, toward a pathology of the subject of objectivity, does not instead open the way in Spinoza toward what might be called a theory of the imaginary: the imaginary being conceived not, as in Descartes, as a psychological category, but as the category through which a world is conceived. In Spinoza the imaginary would no longer be a psychological function, but almost, in the Hegelian sense of the term, an element, that is, a totality into which the psychological functions are integrated and on the basis of which they are constituted. That would be the meaning of the Spinozist distinction of the kinds of knowledge: the imagination isn't a faculty of the mind, it's not a faculty of the psychological subject, the imagination is a world. And when we know that in Spinoza the most remarkable example of the imagination is the example of historical existence, which he describes, for example, in the *Tractatus Theologico-Politicus*, when we see Spinoza relating the functions of psychological subjects, and in particular of prophets, to their function in the world of the imaginary, that is, when we see Spinoza constitute psychological subjects (what we would call psychological subjects) as functions of this world of the imaginary, we may be dealing with a genuine reversal of the problematic of the psychological subject, with a refutation of the problematic of the psychological subject, directly connected with the disappearance in his work of the function of the subject of truth, of the subject of objectivity: that is, we are dealing with the critique of the *cogito*. . . .

What I've said up to this point can be summed up in the following manner: there is no possible psychological subject in Descartes except as a subject of error, that is, as a shadow brought into the pathological by a subject considered as a normal subject, the subject of truth. The question is then the following: why should the truth be expressed, why is it expressed in Descartes in the form of the ego? Why is the truth expressed by the constitution of a subject of truth? Why is there this emergence of a subject of truth as the constitution of truth itself? It's an extremely important phenomenon because it's the origin of the whole of Western philosophy, and the refutation that Spinoza gives of it is a refutation that has disappeared into history, that has been literally submerged by the development of the later problematic, and that has perhaps not yet reemerged except in a lateral and allusive form.

Why is there a subject? . . . Maybe the necessity of having a subject of truth is imposed precisely by Descartes's problematic, which is a problematic that opposes truth to error. It is perhaps in these concepts of truth and error that we find enclosed the requirement of the emergence of a subject as a subject of truth. It is, in fact, entirely striking to see that these concepts of truth and error are the fundamental concepts from which the requirement of a subject of truth emerges. And it is perhaps in the area of the idea of error that we find the meaning of the concept of truth that is opposed to it. What is error, in fact, for a philosophy like that of Descartes? Error is conceived only as the negative other of truth: error is the concept of the nonconcept, but conceived not in its specificity but as the nonconcept of the concept. Error is thought of as reflected on the basis of truth, without, however, this recurrence of truth over error being conceived in its concept. In other words, error is thought of simply as the exterior of a truth, as exclusion from a truth, without the relation to this outside being examined. The relation of error to truth is conceived as a dividing up, that is, as the result of a judgment, as a dividing up that establishes an exclusion, that establishes a condemnation, a dividing up pronounced by the concept of truth itself. But this relationship of exclusion is not examined in the dividing up established between error and truth. In other words, if we can consider that the relation of a truth to the error that it denounces as its own negative reflection manifests not a dividing up but a scission, it is in the misunderstanding of this scission, conceived in the form of a dividing up, that the origin of the emergence of the subject of truth would have its origin. In fact, this relation conceived as a dividing up is the equivalent of a judgment, of a judgment that decides things. And in this judgment that decides things and that consequently misunderstands the scission in the form of a dividing up, we would be dealing with two distinct functions that would not be conceived in their distinction. We would be dealing with the utterance "A is A, non-A is non-A," that is, "the truth is true, error is erroneous," and, on the other hand, we would be dealing (this being a pure utterance, that is, a pure observation) with the judgment that decides things, the judgment that separates, that is, that decides between two values without being reflected otherwise than in the form of judgment. That is to say, a philosophy of judgment like that of Descartes necessarily seems to be necessarily connected with a certain type of relation between a truth and an error conceived in the form of a dividing up—without the act that establishes this dividing up, that is, the foundation of the distinction being examined. A philosophy of judgment would thus be founded on a certain negative relation of truth to error, on a distinction conceived as a dividing up and not as a scission, and it is on that basis that the category of the subject as subject of truth would be established. Obviously, the category of the subject as subject of error is also established on that basis, at once as the pathology of the subject of truth and as its aleatory precondition. And that is how Descartes reflects the whole past of his own philosophy, that is, all the confusion, all the error, that preceded him. Then the question that arises would obviously be why it was necessary that such a philosophy emerge as a philosophy of judgment. In other words, if we can establish the following correlation between truth and error,[24] this scission necessarily leads to a philosophy of judgment, which necessarily leads to a philosophy of the subject that decides between truth and error. Why does the relationship of truth to error bring about the appearance of the subject of truth? The whole problem is why the subject of truth appears to be necessary to conceive the distinction between truth and error. All this resides in the fact that error is conceived as the contrary of truth, as its pure negativity, that is, the fact that the distinction between error and truth, the scission between error and truth, is not examined.

In epistemological retrospection we can clearly assign the difference, we can think what the conditions of the possibility of this distinction were: we can now determine, by historical study, what the conditions of possibility of the distinction between truth and error were. For Descartes, error has a precise content: it's Thomist philosophy, it's Aristotelian physics; the truth is the new physics, it's Galilean physics. All this is the result of a historical process that Descartes does not examine. But we can't explain the appearance of this philosophy, and thus of the subject in which it reflects the judgment that it pronounces on the relation of truth to error, solely by reference to Descartes's illusion. We have to try to account for this function of illusion, for this misunderstanding of a scission that is a historical break, that is, a cultural break, [for this misunderstanding] of the emergence of a new scientific discipline that was conceived in the form of a philosophy of judgment. I can, obviously, only propose a hypothesis: in the philosophy of judgment, Descartes conceived the historical relationship of a new knowledge to an old one in the form of what he had to account for to culture, that is, in a category of the subject of imputation, of the moral subject. That is to say, in a category that is itself caught up in a world of moral imputation: in the world of responsibility. And that's the whole ambiguity of the judge, of judgment: the judge is the one who pronounces a condemnation, who pronounces an exclusion, but in terms such that he can account for them; he's the one who takes the responsibility for deciding on the judgment through which he attributes to one what is his and to the other what is his. In this case we are dealing with a contamination of the ethical categories by the moral and religious categories of the subject of imputation, of the theoretical reflection on the advent of a new scientific discipline.

This could obviously be the object of a historical study: how is it that Descartes felt the need to make a subject of objectivity bear the responsibility for the conception of the advent of a historical event? That probably proceeds from his situation in a world whose objective social structure he did not attempt to conceive, which he did not try to criticize, which he did not try to subject to a critique of the judgment of moral imputation. And it would perhaps not be an accident if Spinoza escapes this category of the subject of imputation projected on the subject of objectivity, precisely insofar as he critiques this moral world in his *Tractatus Theologico-Politicus*, precisely insofar as he critiques the identification of the subjects, critiques the constitution of the subject (psychological subject, ethical subject, and philosophical subject) as being imposed by the structure of the imaginary, that is, by a social structure that necessarily produces this subject in order to be able to subsist.

I think it would be rather simple to show, in a third example much easier to develop, that, starting in the eighteenth century, psychology is always produced by the same schema (since it is in the eighteenth century that psychology is truly born). I believe it would be rather easy to show that the constitution of the psychological subject, the constitution of its functions, that is, the determination of what is to be studied as psychological in a psychological subject from the eighteenth century on, is determined by the dominant philosophy of the eighteenth century: by sensualist empiricism. Starting in the eighteenth century, psychology appears essentially as the by-product of a philosophy of knowledge of a new kind and new style. From that moment on, psychology is not simply the pathological subject of a subject of truth: it becomes the equivalent of philosophy, precisely insofar as sensualist empiricist philosophy identifies the two subjects, identifies the subject of truth and the subject of error in its theory of the empiricist subject. From that moment on, the fundamental problem of perception, the fundamental problem of sensation, enters by rights into psychology, not as a pathological problem, but as a problem of foundation. From that moment on, with the development of the natural sciences and neurophysiology, psychology's relation to physiology enters by rights into psychology, that is, the study of the foundations enters by rights into the perceptive function assigned to the subject by the eighteenth-century empiricist sensualist theory of knowledge. What would be interesting to study in this correlation is the role of language, about which I said something a while ago, precisely insofar as it necessarily appears in connection with the whole eighteenth-century empiricist sensualist theory of knowledge, as having to constitute the very possibility of the objective utterance and as having to resolve the problem that is projected as resolved in the psychological subject instituted by empiricist philosophy. I don't have time to go into detail; I simply want to offer this suggestion.

Consequently, if we want to sum up the fundamental structure that makes it possible for a psychology to exist, I would say that psychology appears to fulfill a twofold function. . . . Psychology appears as the pathology of the theoretical, the moral, the political, or the religious. On the one hand, as [their] pathology and, on the other, as a pathology on which [they can be founded], that is, as a pathology that can be reversed into normalcy. Thus pathology appears as a mirror phenomenon in which the subject of objectivity reflects the possibility of its not being what it is and, at the same time, the possibility of being what it is. In this phenomenon, in which a function is assigned to psychology that is the function the theoretical subject cannot assume, under these conditions, in which psychology appears as responsible for providing the foundation, the function that the theoretical subject, the moral subject, the religious subject, or the political subject delegates to it—in all these cases we are dealing with a veritable mirror function: a mirror of misunderstanding in the form of understanding.[25]

Notes

Foreword

1. Louis Althusser, "Freud and Lacan" (1964–1965, "Freud et Lacan," *La nouvelle Critique*, nos. 161–62), in *Lenin and Philosophy and Other Essays*, trans. Ben Brewster (New York: Monthly Review Press, 1971), pp. 195–220.
2. See for instance Michel Foucault's *The Order of Things: An Archeology of Human Sciences* (*Les mots et les choses, 1966*) (New York: Routledge Classics, 2002).
3. Louis Althusser, "Philosophie et sciences humaines," *Revue de l'enseignement philosophique* 13, no. 5 (June-July 1963). The article was reedited in French in *Solitude de Machiavel et autres textes*, ed. Yves Sintomer (Paris: PUF, 1998), pp. 43–58.
4. See, for instance, the *Rome Discourse* (1953).
5. Michel Foucault, "Foreword," in Georges Canguilhem, *On the Normal and the Pathological*, trans. C. R. Fawcett (Dordrecht: Reidel, 1978), p. 1.
6. Georges Canguilhem, "Qu'est-ce que la psychologie?," *Revue de métaphysique et de morale*, 1958. The article was republished in *Etudes d'histoire et de philosophie des sciences concernant les vivants et la vie* (Paris: Vrin, 1994), pp. 365–81.
7. Cf. Jacques Lacan's paper entitled *The Subversion of the Subject and the Dialectic of Desire in the Freudian Unconscious* (1960).

8. *Idéologie et appareils idéologiques d'Etat* (*La Pensée*, 1970). English edition: *Ideology and Ideological State Apparatuses* (*IISA*), in *Lenin and Philosophy and Other Essays*, trans. Ben Brewster (New York: Monthly Review Press, 1971).

9. Cf. Louis Althusser, *For Marx*, trans. Ben Brewster (New York: Verso, 2005), part 7, 4, p. 232.

10. Ibid., p. 231.

11. Cf. *IISA*, pp. 170–82.

12. Cf. Lacan's seminar 2, "The Ego in Freud's Theory and in the Technique of Psychoanalysis" (1954–1955).

13. Cf Foucault, *The Order of Things,* ch. 10, 5, "Psychoanalysis and Ethnology," pp. 407–11. According to Foucault, psychoanalysis, with the concept of the unconscious, introduces a "principle of dissatisfaction" within the field of the human sciences.

Editors' Preface

1. Cf. our presentation of Louis Althusser's *Écrits sur la psychanalyse: Freud et Lacan* (Paris: Stock/IMEC, 1983, Le Livre de Poche, 1995); cf. also Elisabeth Roudinesco, *Jacques Lacan: Esquisse d'une vie, histoire d'un système de pensée* (Paris: Fayard, 1993).

2. The recording of this speech and all the documents quoted in this edition are in Althusser's archives and can be consulted at the Institut Mémoires de l'édition contemporaine (IMEC).

3. "Freud et Lacan," *La Nouvelle Critique* (December 1964-January 1965), rpt. in Althusser, *Écrits sur la psychanalyse.*

4. This chronology is based on a double set of manuscript notes taken by members of the audience, Althusser's notes preserved in his archives, and Étienne Balibar's notes, which he desposited at the IMEC. Althusser's archives also contain the recordings of the following presentations: Althusser's second presentation (almost complete), complete presentations by Étienne Balibar and Jacques-Alain Miller, and Michel Tort's presentation (short fragment).

These recordings also contain, following the presentations, a certain number of discussions in which Althusser played an important part.

1. The Place of Psychoanalysis in the Human Sciences

1. A founding member of the Société psychanalytique de Paris, Angelo Hesnard was the author, with Emmanuel Regis, of the first book on psychoanalysis published in France: *La Psychanalyse des névroses et des psychoses, ses applications médicales et extra-médicales* (Paris: Alcan, 1914). His book, *L'oeuvre de Freud* (Paris: Payot, 1960) included a preface by Maurice Merleau-Ponty. He died in 1969.

2. In the absence of any other source, we follow here the text of the transcription.

3. Roland Dalbiez was the author of a book that was famous in its time: *La Méthode psychanalytique freudienne* (Paris: Desclée de Brouwer, 1936). It sought to separate psychoanalytic technique, which he regarded as innovative, from Freudian doctrine, which he regarded as a confused philosophy. He had considerable influence: one of his students was Paul Ricoeur.

4. Althusser is referring essentially to Georges Politzer's *Critique des fondements de la psychologie* (Paris: Rieder, 1928). An exchange of letters with Guy Besse, then director of Éditions Sociales, shows that in June 1955 Althusser planned to republish Politzer's work, preceded by a "theoretical preface," in the future Theorie series. Learning from Guy Besse that Presses Universitaires de France was planning to publish the text "simply accompanied by a biographical note," Althusser wrote to him, for example, on June 23, 1965:

> Is it really too late to try to resume the project? I'm talking to you about it again for a reason whose *gravity* cannot be overestimated, namely: Politzer's text, put before the public *without a theoretical preface* that every reader would be obliged to read is going to cause great *damage*. Even if we publish elsewhere, and in time,

a theoretical-critical text on the *Critique of Foundations*, how many readers of the *Critique* will read our text? They will launch into the *Critique,* and the results will be, we can safely predict, *disastrous.* The *Critique* is a brilliant text, but it is wrong, and profoundly idealist. His genius is to have understood Freud's crucial importance at a time when it was suspected by almost no one in France—his mistake was to have given an exposition and critique of it that was *100% idealist,* and very precisely existentialist. It was not by wrongly interpreting Politzer that Sartre and Merleau used it in the way we know: it was, unfortunately, by *correctly interpreting* Politzer: Sartre's only teacher is Politzer, his only true teacher (with . . . as paradoxical as it may seem, Bergson! In his work the influence of Husserl is much more superficial, despite his numerous terminological borrowings from him).

Politzer's book was finally republished by PUF in 1967.

5. "Lacan's society" is the Société française de psychanalyse, founded by Daniel Lagache in June 1953; the "old one" is the Société psychanalytique de Paris; created in 1926, it was then headed by Sacha Nacht.

6. Two issues of the *Revue de psychologie concrète* were in fact published in 1929.

7. This seems to refer to the report delivered by Jean Laplanche and Serge Leclaire to the Bonneval colloquium. Althusser had an unsigned offprint of this report: J. Laplanche and S. Leclaire: "L'inconscient. Une étude psychanalytique," *Les Temps modernes,* July 1961.

8. The transcript, which is probably in conformity with what Althusser said, gives *psychanalyse* (psychoanalysis). However, it is likely that Althusser meant *psychologie concrète.*

9. The transcript and the listener's notes give *sociologie.* However, we can assume that Althusser meant to say *psychologie* here.

10. Analyzed by Freud, Abram Kardiner was one of the representatives of the "culturalist" trend. See, for example, *The Individual and His Society: The Psychodynamics of Primitive Social Organization* (New York: Columbia University Press, 1939), and *My Analysis with Freud: Reminiscences* (New York: Norton, 1977).

11. In fact, he was Viennese in origin. Before emigrating to the United States, René Spitz took an active part in the Société psychanalytique de Paris. He is famous for his works on the observation of infants and on "hospitalism." See, for example, *The First Year of Life: A Psychoanalytic Study of Normal and Deviant Development of Object Relations* (New York: International Universities Press, 1965).

12. Here Althusser is referring to the article "Comment se développe la notion de corps propre chez l'enfant," *Journal de Psychologie* (November-December 1931), in which Henri Wallon develops the idea of the "trial of the mirror"; the article was republished in his book *Les Origines du caractère chez l'enfant* (Paris: Bovin, 1934). In 1936 Jacques Lacan presented his own conception of the "mirror stage" at the Marienbad Congress of the International Psychoanalytic Association. Most of this text, which had not been published, was incorporated in 1938 into Lacan's contribution to volume 8 of *L'Encyclopédie française,* which was edited by Wallon ("La Famille"). When in July 1949 he gave his famous talk on the "mirror stage" at the Zurich Congress ("La stade du miroir comme formateur de la fonction du Je," republished in his *Écrits* [Paris: PUF, 1985], pp. 93–100) Lacan in fact omitted any reference to Wallon.

13. The transcript reads *sociologie.* Althusser may have meant to say *société.*

14. According to Descartes, the "pineal gland" is the point in the brain where the "most peculiar union of the soul with part of the body" takes place.

15. Without naming her, Lacan calls Melanie Klein a "tripe butcher and brilliant woman." Lacan, *Écrits.*

16. Anna Freud, *Mécanisme de défense du moi,* 11th ed. (Paris: PUF, 1985) and *La Psychanalyse des enfants,* 4th ed. (Paris: PUF, 1981).

17. A representative of "American neo-Freudianism," Franz Alexander founded the Chicago Institute for Psychoanalysis in 1931. See for example his *Psychosomatic Medicine: Its Principles and Applications,* 2d ed. (New York: Norton, 1987).

18. This was a colloquium held at Bonneval from October 30 to November 2, 1960. Acta published in the *VIe colloque de Bonneval: l'inconscient* (Paris: Desclée de Brouwer, 1966).

19. A classmate of Lacan's at Sainte-Anne and his friend, Henri Ey succeeded René Laforgue as leader of the L'évolution psychiatrique group, seeking to organize a confrontation between psychiatry and psychoanalysis. In 1933 he took charge of the psychiatric hospital at Bonneval, which he did not leave until 1970.

20. J. H. Jackson (1835–1911): a British neurologist, famous in particular for his works on epilepsy and aphasia and more generally for his research on the relations between thought and the brain. Henri Ey is often considered one of the principal representatives of the "neo-Jacksonian" current in psychiatry.

21. For details, see Élisabeth Roudinesco, *La Bataille de cent ans: Histoire de la psychanalyse en France,* vol. 2 (Paris: Seuil, 1986), pp. 317–28; and Jacques Lacan, *Esquisse d'une vie, histoire d'un système de pensée* (Paris: Fayard, 1993), pp. 383–403.

22. The transcript gives only "mon maître J."

23. A member of the Viennese Psychoanalytic Society since 1908, Ludwig Binswanger directed the Bellevue Sanatorium in Switzerland from 1911 to 1956. Strongly influenced by phenomenology, he was the inventor of "existential psychoanalysis" (*Dasein-analyse*). See, in English, *Being in the World: Selected Papers of Ludwig Binswanger,* trans. Jacob Needleman (London: Souvenir, 1975).

24. *La Psychanalyse,* no. 1: *Sur la parole et le langage* (Paris: PUF, 1956). Texts reprinted in Lacan, *Écrits,* pp. 369–99 and 879–87.

2. Psychoanalysis and Psychology

"Psychoanalysis and Psychology" is the title given by Louis Althusser.

1. Sigmund Freud, *An Outline of Psychoanalysis* (New York: Norton, 1989).
2. Jacques Lacan, "La direction de la cure et les principes de son pouvoir," *La Psychanalyse*, no. 6, reprinted in *Écrits* (Paris: Seuil, 1966), pp. 623ff.
3. See the preface to this volume.
4. Cf. the preface to this volume.
5. Althusser is referring to a schema drawn on the blackboard.
6. Lucien Malson, *Les Enfants sauvages* (Paris: 10/18, 1964).
7. Cf. René Spitz, *La Première année de la vie de l'enfant* (Paris: PUF, 1963).
8. Located at no. 254 rue Saint-Jacques, this institute is now called the Institut national des jeunes sourds.
9. In Malson, *Les Enfants sauvages,* pp. 161–62.
10. A reference to the schema drawn on the blackboard.
11. Cf. Maurice Halbwachs, *Les Cadres sociaux de la mémoire*, rev. ed. (Paris: Albin Michel, 1994).
12. *Revue française de la psychanalyse* (July-September 1956).
13. A literal transcript of the recording would yield approximately the following text: "The whole attempt made by Melanie Freud . . . by Anna Freud [laughter in the audience]. I try to go beyond my colleagues."
14. Anna Freud, "La contribution de la psychanalyse à la psychologie génétique," *Revue française de psychanalyse* (July-September 1956): 376.
15. Ibid., p. 371.
16. Instead of "Melanie Klein," which is what Althusser actually said.
17. Cf. the preceding note.
18. Ibid.
19. Jacques Lacan, "Fonction et champ de la parole et du langage," *La Psychanalyse* 1 (1956): "Actes du Congrès de Rome, 26 et 27 septembre 1953" (reprinted in *Écrits,* pp. 237–322). Daniel Lagache's paper is published on pages 211–20 of the same volume.

20. The recording gives "Mélanie Freud" here.
21. *Écrits,* p. 217. In "Rome Discourse," Lacan mentions here Michaël Balint and "the slogan that he borrows from Rickman, the advent of a *Two body psychology*" (ibid., p. 304).
22. The author of a *Traité de psychologie* published in 1750.
23. Christian Wolff, an eighteenth-century German philosopher said to be the first to use the term *psychology*.
24. Reference to a schema on the blackboard.
25. The recording stops in the middle of the following sentence.

Index

abstract concepts, 15, 17

Alexander, Franz, 28–29, 94*n*17

Althusser, Louis, viii–ix, xvi–xvii, xxii, xxxii, 93*nn*7–8; with "interpellation into subject," xxiii; letter to Besse, 91*n*4; with seminars, vii, xxxi, xxxiii–xxxiv

"American neo-Freudianism," 94*n*17

"American psychoanalysis," xv, xix–xx, 27

Anthropologie structurale (Lévi-Strauss), 31

anthropology: anthropologism, x, xiv, xv, xx, xxv, xxix; psychoanalysis and, 21, 30, 46; structural anthropology, 31; "wild children" and, xxiv, 51–57

Aveyron. *See* wild boy of Aveyron

Bachelard, Gaston, xx

Balibar, Étienne, xxxi, xxxii, xxxiii, 91*n*4

Balint, Michaël, 96*n*21

behavior, morals and, 67, 69, 73, 74

Bellevue Sanatorium, 95*n*23

Bergson, Henri, 34, 92; Bergsonian spiritualism, x; Bergsonism, ix, 35

Besse, Guy, 91*n*4

Binswanger, Ludwig, 39, 95*n*23

biology: with becoming-human, 50–60, 62, 64; biological theory, 6; culture and, 59–60; psychoanalysis and, 30, 31, 42; psychophysiology and, 22–23, 42

Bonnet, Charles, 75

Bonneval colloquium, 93*n*7, 94*n*18

Bourdieu, Pierre, xxxi

Canguilhem, Georges, xiii

Capital (Marx), xx, xxxi, xxxiv

Charcot, Jean-Martin, 4

Chicago Institute for Psychoanalysis, 94*n*17

Chiesa, Achille, xxxiii

children, 93*n*12; child development,
xiv, 22; child psychology, 21,
22; "hospitalism" and, 93*n*11;
humanization process and,
xxiii–xxiv, 51, 62, 64; maturation
and, 25–26; oedipal moment and,
50; psychoanalysis of, xiv, 20, 25;
reality principle and, 25–26; "wild
children," xxiv, 51–57
civilization, neurosis of, 4–5
Civilization and Its Discontents (S.
Freud), 21, 47
classical psychology. *See* psychology
cogito, xxvi, xxix, 77, 79, 80
concepts: abstract, 15, 17; conceptualization, of ideology, xxii; domestic, 7; Freud, Sigmund, with, 5–7,
16; imported, 5–7; nonconcept
and, 15, 17, 42–43, 78, 82
concrete psychology, xiii, 15, 16
Condillac, Étienne Bonnot de, 51, 53,
56, 62
consciousness: ego and, 66; id and,
16, 71; philosophy of, ix, xiii,
xxix, 69, 71; psychology of, xvii,
49, 70; theoretical consciousness,
27–28, 38, 42; with unconscious,
16, 18
*Critique des fondements de la psycholo-
gie* (Politzer), xii–xiii, 14, 91*n*4
culture: biology and, 59–60; "culturalist" trend, 93*n*10; cultural

phenomena, 21; law of culture,
xxiii, xxiv, 60; nature and, xxiv–
xxv, 51–52; precession of culture,
xxiv, xxv, 63

Dalbiez, Roland, 12, 91*n*3
Darwin, Charles, 6
Descartes, René, 27; error and,
xxviii, 81–84; pineal gland and,
94*n*14; with psychology,
76–77, 78, 81; Spinoza and,
xxvi–xxvii, 79–80; subject and,
xxviii–xxix
dialectical psychology, 23
didactic psychoanalysis, 8–9
*Discours sur l'origine et les fondements
de l'ingalitéparmi les hommes*
(Rousseau), xxiv, 61
dissatisfaction, principle of, 90*n*13
doctors: drama and, 34; patients and,
xvi, 32, 33, 34, 39, 70
Dolto, Françoise, 28
double personality, 66–67
drama: as abstract concept, 17; with
doctor and patient, 34; psychology and, 15–16, 70
Duroux, Yves, xxxiii–xxxiv

Écolenormalesupérieure (ENS),
vii, xxxi
economy: economic theory, xxi, 6;
political economy, xx, 6, 30

Ecrits sur la psychanalyse: Freud et Lacan (Althusser), xxii

ego: centrality of, xix, 67–68, 71; consciousness and, 66; *ego cogito*, 77, 79; Freud, Anna, and, 27–28, 66, 67–69; the imaginary with ego structure, 71–72; nonconcept and, 78; with psychology, structures of, 73–74; resistance and, 68; superego, 25, 27, 29, 30, 66–67

empiricism, ix, 86–87

Encyclopédiefrançaise, L', 93*n*12

energy theory, in physics, 6

Enfantssauvages, Les, 51

Engels, Friedrich, xxi

ENS (École normale supérieure), vii, xxxi

epistemological break, xvii, xx, xxi, 48

epithumía, 76

error: nonconcept and, 82; truth and, xxvii, xxviii, 78–79, 81–84

Ethics (Spinoza), xxvii

"existential psychoanalysis," 39, 95*n*23

Ey, Henri, 34–35, 36, 94*nn*19–20

Feuerbach, Ludwig, xx

first-person knowledge, 34

fondement en miroir (mirror foundation), 75

"for-others" (*Mitsein*), 39

Foucault, Michel, xxix–xxx; with dissatisfaction, principle of,

90*n*13; with phenomenology and structural analysis, xiii

France, 65, 91*n*4, 92*n*5; *L'Encyclopédiefrançaise,* 93*n*12; Freud, Sigmund, with philosophy and reception in, xii–xvi, 3–4; provincialism and, 11

Freud, Anna, xix, 22, 96*n*13; double personality and, 66–67; ego and, 27–28, 66, 67–69; with psychology and psychoanalysis, 65–66

Freud, Sigmund, xxviii, 20; "American neo-Freudianism," 94*n*17; with concepts, 5–7, 16; criticism of, 3–4; influence, xxi, xxix, 18, 19, 21, 47–49, 91*nn*3–4; Lacan on, 45; on neurosis, 4–5; psychoanalysis and, xii–xvi, 45, 46; psychological resistance and, 3–7; reality principle and, 24–26; reception in French philosophy, xii–xvi, 3–4; unconscious and, xi, xix, xxii, xxix, 70

"Freud et Lacan" (Althusser), vii, xvi, xxii, xxxii

Future of an Illusion, The (Freud, S.), 21, 47

Galileo, 18, 48, 84

German Ideology, The (Engels and Marx), xxi

Guitton, Jean, 38

Halbwachs, Maurice, 64

Hegel, Georg Wilhelm Friedrich, xx, 17, 80

Hesnard, Angelo, 3, 12, 91*n*1

Hobbes, Thomas, 60–61

homo oeconomicus, xvii, xxv

homo psychologicus, xvi, xxv

"hospitalism," 93*n*11

humans: biology and becoming-human, 50–60, 62, 64; human-ization-subjectivization process, xxiii–xxiv, 51, 62, 64. *See also* children

human sciences, xxv; with dissatisfaction, principle of, 90*n*13; philosophical issue with question of, vii, viii–xii, xvi, xvii, xx; psychoanalysis and, xviii, 1–3, 20–21, 44; with scientificity, lack of, ix; scientific status of, xxx

Hyppolite, Jean, 40

id, xix, 16, 66, 67, 68, 69, 71

ideology: conceptualization of, xxii; defined, xxiii; ideological philosophy, viii, x; moral, 75; political, 75; psychology and, 74–75; technocratic ideology, x, xxv; theory, premises to, xxi–xxx

Ideology and Ideological State Apparatuses (Althusser), xxii

the imaginary: ego structure with, 71–72; materialism of, xxii, 80; theory, 58, 80

IMEC (Institut Mémoires de l'édition contemporaine), 90*n*2, 91*n*4

individual: politics with morals in, 77; with psychology, structures of, 73–74

Institut Mémoires de l'édition contemporaine (IMEC), 90*n*2, 91*n*4

Institut national des jeunes sourds, 95*n*8

intellectual terrorism, 40–41

International Psychoanalytic Association, 93*n*12

"interpellation into subject," xxiii

intersubjectivity, philosophy of, xvi, 37, 39

Italy, provincialism and, 11

Itard, Jean Marc Gaspard, 60; language and, 53–58; with wild boy of Aveyron, 51–55

Jackson, J. H., 34, 35, 94*n*20

judgment, philosophy of, xxvii, 83, 84–85

Kant, Immanuel, 5–6

Kardiner, Abram, 21, 93*n*10

Klein, Melanie, 22, 28, 94*n*15, 96*n*16

knowledge: theory of, 86–87; third-person and first-person, 34; truth and, xxvi–xxvii, 48

Lacan, Jacques, xxii, 96*n*21; "American psychoanalysis" and, 27; on Ey, 35–36; on Freud, Sigmund, 45; influence, xvii, xxiv, 13, 39–41, 69–70; with intellectual terrorism, 40–41; on Klein, 94*n*15; Lacan seminar (1963–1964), vii, xxxi, xxxii, xxxiii–xxxiv, 40–41; "Lacan's society" and, 92*n*5; law of culture and, 60; with "mirror stage," 23, 93*n*12; nonconcept and, 42–43; philosophy and, xvi–xxi, 33, 39–40; psychoanalysis and, 45–46, 50; with psychology, xiii, xv; Rousseau and, xxiv–xxv; subject and, xxviii–xxix
Laforgue, René, 94*n*19
Lagache, Daniel, 69–70, 92*n*5, 96*n*19
language, xii; Italy and foreign-language translations, 11; with knowledge, theory of, 86–87; linguistics and, xii, xxi, xxv, xxx; signs and, 57–58, 64; "wild children" and, 53–57
Laplanche, Jean, 16, 36, 39, 93*n*7
law of culture, xxiii, xxiv, 60
Leclaire, Serge, 36, 93*n*7

letter, from Althusser to Besse, 91*n*4
Lévi-Strauss, Claude, 31
linguistics, xii, xxi; modern, xxv; as real science, xxx
Lire Le Capital (Althusser, Balibar, Rancière, and Macherey), xxxi, xxxii
Little Hans (Freud, S.), 20

Macherey, Pierre, xxxi, xxxii
madness, 31, 35
Malinowski, Bronislaw, 30
Malson, Lucien, 51
Marx, Karl, xviii; influence, 23, 44; Marx seminar (1961–1962), xxxi; Marx seminar (1964), xxxi, xxxiv; "return to Marx," vii, xx, xxi
maturation: psychological, 23; types of, 25–26
Mead, Margaret, 21
Mécanisme de défense du moi (A. Freud), 28
medicine. *See* psychosomatic medicine
Meditations on First Philosophy (Descartes), xxviii
Merleau-Ponty, Maurice, ix, xxxiii, 40, 91*n*1; influence, xii, 12, 14; influences on, 91*n*4; with philosophy and psychoanalysis, xv–xvi, 12, 13, 14, 33

Méthode psychanalytique freudienne, La (Dalbiez), 91*n*3
military analogy, therapy and, 8
Miller, Jacques-Alain, xxxiii, 91*n*4
mirrors: mirror foundation or *fondement en miroir*, 75; "mirror stage," 23, 93*n*12; pathology as mirror phenomenon, 87; "trial of the mirror," 93*n*12; "wild children" with, 52
Mitsein ("for-others"), 39
Monde, Le, 29
morals, 87; behavior and, 67, 69, 73, 74; ideology, 75; moral world, 84, 85; with politics, 77
Mosconi, Jean, xxxiv

Nacht, Sacha, 13, 92*n*5
nature: culture and, xxiv–xxv, 51–52; society and, 60–62
neurology, 23, 25, 31, 42
neurosis, of civilization, 4–5
nonconcept, 17; of classical psychology, 15; ego and, 78; error and, 82; Lacan and, 42–43
noûs, 76

oedipal moment, 25, 50
Order of Things, The (Foucault), xxix–xxx
Origines du caractère chez l'enfant, Les (Wallon), 93*n*12

Passeron, Jean-Claude, xxxi
pathology: as mirror phenomenon, 87; psychology and, 76–81, 83, 86
patients: doctors and, xvi, 33, 34, 39, 70; drama and, 34
phenomenology, xxxiii, 72; influence, xxxiv, 95*n*23; "pseudo phenomenology," x; role of, ix, xii; structural analysis and, xiii
Phenomenology of Mind (Hegel), 17
philosophy: of consciousness, ix, xiii, xxix, 69, 71; Freud, Sigmund, reception in French philosophy, xii–xvi, 3–4; with human sciences, question of, vii, viii–xii, xvi, xvii, xx; ideological philosophy, viii, x; of intersubjectivity, xvi, 37, 39; of judgment, xxvii, 83, 84–85; Lacan and, xvi–xxi, 33, 39–40; psychiatry and, 36; psychoanalysis and, xv–xvi, xx, 12–14, 31–33, 39; psychology and, viii, 86
"Philosophy and the Human Sciences" (Althusser), viii–ix, xvi, xvii
physics: energy theory in, 6; Galileo and, 18, 48, 84
pineal gland, 26, 27, 30–31, 94*n*14
Plato, 75–77
politics, 80, 85; morals and, 77; Plato and political problem, 76–77; political economy, xx, 6, 30; political ideology, 75

Politzer, Georges, xii–xiii, 12, 42, 70; influence, 13, 14, 91*n*4; on psychology, 14–17, 18, 34
positivism, ix
Pour Marx (Althusser), xxxi
pragmatism, ix
precession of culture. *See* culture
Presses Universitaires de France (PUF), 91*n*4
provincialism, 11, 34
"pseudo phenomenology," x
pseudo science, xi, xxx, 14
Psychanalyse, La, 40
Psychanalyse des enfants, La (Freud, A.), 28
Psychanalyse des névroses et des psychoses, ses applications médicales et extra-médicales, La (Hesnard and Regis), 91*n*1
psychiatry, xiv, xv, 23; Ey and, 34–35, 94*n*20; philosophy and, 36; psychoanalysis and, 20, 21, 38–39, 44, 94*n*19
psychoanalysis, 91*n*3, 92*n*5, 93*n*11; "American psychoanalysis," xv, xix–xx, 27; anthropology and, 21, 30, 46; biology and, 30, 31, 42; Chicago Institute for Psychoanalysis, 94*n*17; of children, xiv, 20, 25; didactic psychoanalysis, 8–9; "existential psychoanalysis," 39, 95*n*23; Freud, Sigmund, and, xii–xvi, 45, 46; human sciences and, xviii, 1–3, 20–21, 44; Lacan and, 45–46, 50; philosophy and, xv–xvi, xx, 12–14, 31–33, 39; as practice instead of science, xv–xvi, 7–8; psychiatry and, 20, 21, 38–39, 44, 94*n*19; psychological resistance with, 3–7; psychology and, xiii–xv, xx, xxxiii, 14–16, 19–20, 22–24, 31, 37–39, 45–50, 65–71; reality principle and, 25, 29–30, 67–68; shaman as psychoanalyst, 31; society and, 31; theory as inadequate, 10–11; therapy with, 7–8, 10; truth through, 8; as "two-body psychology," 70; unconscious and, xii, 90*n*13
"Psychoanalysis and Phenomenology" (Duroux), xxxiii–xxxiv
"Psychoanalysis and Psychology" conference, xx
psychology, xii, 91*n*4; child psychology, 21, 22; classical psychology, xiii, 14, 15, 16, 17, 22, 23, 69; concrete, xiii, 15, 16; of consciousness, xvii, 49, 70; criticism of, xiii–xiv; Descartes with, 76–77, 78, 81; dialectical, 23; drama and, 15–16, 70; ideology and, 74–75; pathology and, 76–81, 83, 86; philosophy and, viii, 86; Politzer on, 14–17, 18, 34; as pseudo science, xxx, 14;

psychology (*continued*)
psychoanalysis and, xiii–xv, xx, xxxiii, 14–16, 19–20, 22–24, 31, 37–39, 45–50, 65–71; psychoanalysis as "two-body psychology," 70; psychological maturation, 23; psychological resistance, 3–7; psychologism and, vii, ix; structures of, 72–75; unconscious and, 18, 49, 64, 71; Wolff and, 75, 96*n*23
psychophysiology, 22–23, 42
psychosociology, xi, 51
psychosomatic medicine, 20
psychotherapy, 20, 33, 38
PUF (Presses Universitaires de France), 91*n*4

"radical transcendence of the Subject," ix
Rancière, Jacques, xxxi, xxxii
reality principle: children and, 25–26; defined, 24–25; psychoanalysis and, 25, 29–30, 67–68; society and, 24–26, 27
recollection, 63, 64
recurrence, 62, 63–64
Regis, Emmanuel, 91*n*1
Republic, The (Plato), 75, 76
resistance: to concepts, imported, 5–7; ego and, 68; psychological resistance, 3–7
Revue de l'enseignement philosophique, viii

Revue de psychologie concrète, 15, 93*n*6
Revue française de psychanalyse, 65
Rickman, John, 96*n*21
Ricoeur, Paul, xii, xvi, 36–37, 91*n*3
"Rome Discourse" (Lacan), 69, 96*n*21
Rousseau, Jean-Jacques: Hobbes and, 60–61; Lacan and, xxiv–xxv

Sartre, Jean-Paul, ix, 69; with "existential psychoanalysis," 39; influence, xii, 14; influences on, 91*n*4; oedipal moment and, 25; with philosophy and psychoanalysis, xv–xvi, 12, 13, 14, 33
science: pseudo science, xi, xxx, 14; with psychoanalysis and psychology, 19–20; psychoanalysis as practice instead of, xv–xvi, 7–8. *See also* human sciences
seminars: Bourdieu and Passeron seminar (1963), xxxi; Lacan seminar (1963–1964), vii, xxxi, xxxii, xxxiii–xxxiv, 40–41; Marx seminar (1961–1962), xxxi; Marx seminar (1964), xxxi, xxxiv; structuralism seminar (1962–1963), xxxi
shaman, as psychoanalyst, 31
signs, language and, 57–58, 64
Société française de psychanalyse, 92*n*5

Société psychanalytique de Paris,
92*n*5, 93*n*11
society: "Lacan's society" and, 92*n*5;
madness and, 31, 35; nature and,
60–62; Plato with structure of,
75–77; psychoanalysis and, 31;
reality principle and, 24–26, 27;
social praxis and, 26–27; superego
and, 30
Spinoza, Baruch, 85; Descartes and,
xxvi–xxvii, 79–80; *Ethics* by,
xxvii; with imaginary, materialism of, xxii, 80; influence, xxix;
knowledge and, xxvii
spiritualism, viii, x
Spitz, René, 22, 52, 93*n*11
structure: phenomenology and
structural analysis, xiii; Plato
with structure of society, 75–77;
psychology, structure of, 72–75;
structural anthropology, 31; structuralism seminar (1962–1963),
xxxi
subject: Descartes and, xxviii–xxix;
humanization-subjectivization
process, xxiii–xxiv, 51, 62, 64;
"interpellation into subject," xxiii;
philosophy of intersubjectivity, xvi, 37, 39; with psychology,
structures of, 73–75
superego, 25, 27, 29, 30, 66–67
surrealism, 40

technocratic ideology, x, xxv
terrorism. *See* intellectual terrorism
theory: biological, 6; economic, xxi,
6; energy theory in physics, 6; of
ideology, premises to, xxi–xxx;
the imaginary, 58, 80; inadequacy
of psychoanalytic, 10–11; of
knowledge, 86–87; pineal gland,
30; theoretical consciousness,
27–28, 38, 42; of unconscious, xix,
xxii, 16, 64
therapy, 64; military analogy and,
8; with psychoanalysis, 7–8, 10;
psychotherapy, 20, 33, 38
third-person knowledge, 34
Three Essays on Sexuality (S. Freud), 20
thumós, 76
Tort, Michel, xxxiii, 16, 20, 24, 91*n*4
Totem and Taboo (Freud, S.), 21, 47
Tractatus Theologico-Politicus
(Spinoza), 80, 85
Traite des passions de l'âme (Descartes), 78, 79–80
transcendence: "radical transcendence of the Subject," ix; of
unconscious, 71–72
*Treatise on the Emendation of the
Intellect* (Spinoza), xxvii
"trial of the mirror." *See* mirror
truth: error and, xxvii, xxviii, 78–79,
81–84; knowledge and, xxvi–xxvii,
48; through psychoanalysis, 8

unconscious, 28, 36; consciousness with, 16, 18; Freud, Sigmund, and, xi, xix, xxii, xxix, 70; psychoanalysis and, xii, 90*n*13; psychology and, 18, 49, 64, 71; theory of, xix, xxii, 16, 64; transcendence of, 71–72

Victor. *See* wild boy of Aveyron

Wallon, Henri, 22–24, 93*n*12
wild boy of Aveyron (Victor), 51–57
"wild children." *See* children
Wolff, Christian, 75, 96*n*23

Zurich Congress, 93*n*12

Carlo Ginzburg, *Wooden Eyes: Nine Reflections on Distance*

Sylviane Agacinski, *Parity of the Sexes*

Michel Pastoureau, *The Devil's Cloth: A History of Stripes and Striped Fabric*

Alain Cabantous, *Blasphemy: Impious Speech in the West from the Seventeenth to the Nineteenth Century*

Julia Kristeva, *The Sense and Non-Sense of Revolt: The Powers and Limits of Psychoanalysis*

Kelly Oliver, *The Portable Kristeva*

Gilles Deleuze, *Dialogues II*

Catherine Clément and Julia Kristeva, *The Feminine and the Sacred*

Sylviane Agacinski, *Time Passing: Modernity and Nostalgia*

Luce Irigaray, *Between East and West: From Singularity to Community*

Julia Kristeva, *Hannah Arendt*

Julia Kristeva, *Intimate Revolt: The Powers and Limits of Psychoanalysis*, vol. 2

Elisabeth Roudinesco, *Why Psychoanalysis?*

Régis Debray, *Transmitting Culture*

Steve Redhead, ed., *The Paul Virilio Reader*

Claudia Benthien, *Skin: On the Cultural Border Between Self and the World*

Julia Kristeva, *Melanie Klein*

Roland Barthes, *The Neutral: Lecture Course at the Collège de France (1977–1978)*

Hélène Cixous, *Portrait of Jacques Derrida as a Young Jewish Saint*

Theodor W. Adorno, *Critical Models: Interventions and Catchwords*

Julia Kristeva, *Colette*

Gianni Vattimo, *Dialogue with Nietzsche*

Emmanuel Todd, *After the Empire: The Breakdown of the American Order*

Gianni Vattimo, *Nihilism and Emancipation: Ethics, Politics, and Law*

Hélène Cixous, *Dream I Tell You*

Steve Redhead, *The Jean Baudrillard Reader*

Jean Starobinski, *Enchantment: The Seductress in Opera*

Jacques Derrida, *Geneses, Genealogies, Genres, and Genius: The Secrets of the Archive*

Hélène Cixous, *White Ink: Interviews on Sex, Text, and Politics*

Marta Segarra, ed., *The Portable Cixous*

François Dosse, *Gilles Deleuze and Félix Guattari: Intersecting Lives*

Julia Kristeva, *This Incredible Need to Believe*

François Noudelmann, *The Philosopher's Touch: Sartre, Nietzsche, and Barthes at the Piano*

Antoine de Baecque, *Camera Historica: The Century in Cinema*

Julia Kristeva, *Hatred and Forgiveness*

Roland Barthes, *How to Live Together: Novelistic Simulations of Some Everyday Spaces*

Jean-Louis Flandrin and Massimo Montanari, *Food: A Culinary History*

Georges Vigarello, *The Metamorphoses of Fat: A History of Obesity*

Julia Kristeva, *The Severed Heads: Capital Visions*

Eelco Runia, *Moved by the Past: Discontinuity and Historical Mutation*

François Hartog, *Regimes of Historicity: Presentism and Experiences of Time*

Jacques Le Goff, *Must We Divide History Into Periods?*

Claude Lévi-Strauss, *We Are All Cannibals: And Other Essays*

Marc Augé, *Everyone Dies Young: Time Without Age*